Apress Pocket Guides

Apress Pocket Guides present concise summaries of cutting-edge developments and working practices throughout the tech industry. Shorter in length, books in this series aims to deliver quick-to-read guides that are easy to absorb, perfect for the time-poor professional.

This series covers the full spectrum of topics relevant to the modern industry, from security, AI, machine learning, cloud computing, web development, product design, to programming techniques and business topics too.

Typical topics might include:

- A concise guide to a particular topic, method, function or framework

- Professional best practices and industry trends

- A snapshot of a hot or emerging topic

- Industry case studies

- Concise presentations of core concepts suited for students and those interested in entering the tech industry

- Short reference guides outlining 'need-to-know' concepts and practices.

More information about this series at https://link.springer.com/bookseries/17385.

Secure RESTful APIs

Simple Solutions for Beginners

Massimo Nardone

Apress®

Secure RESTful APIs: Simple Solutions for Beginners

Massimo Nardone
Helsinki, Finland

ISBN-13 (pbk): 979-8-8688-1284-2   ISBN-13 (electronic): 979-8-8688-1285-9
https://doi.org/10.1007/979-8-8688-1285-9

Managing Director, Apress Media LLC: Welmoed Spahr
Acquisitions Editor: Melissa Duffy
Development Editor: Laura Berendson
Editorial Assistant: Gryffin Winkler

Cover designed by eStudioCalamar

Distributed to the book trade worldwide by Springer Science+Business Media New York, 1 New York Plaza, Suite 4600, New York, NY 10004-1562, USA. Phone 1-800-SPRINGER, fax (201) 348-4505, e-mail orders-ny@springer-sbm.com, or visit www.springeronline.com. Apress Media, LLC is a California LLC and the sole member (owner) is Springer Science + Business Media Finance Inc (SSBM Finance Inc). SSBM Finance Inc is a **Delaware** corporation.

For information on translations, please e-mail booktranslations@springernature.com; for reprint, paperback, or audio rights, please e-mail bookpermissions@springernature.com.

Apress titles may be purchased in bulk for academic, corporate, or promotional use. eBook versions and licenses are also available for most titles. For more information, reference our Print and eBook Bulk Sales web page at http://www.apress.com/bulk-sales.

Any source code or other supplementary material referenced by the author in this book is available to readers on GitHub. For more detailed information, please visit https://www.apress.com/gp/services/source-code.

If disposing of this product, please recycle the paper

This book is dedicated to the memory of my loving late father Giuseppe. Your support, your education, your values made me the man I am now. You will be loved and missed forever. I also would like to dedicate this book to my children Luna, Leo and Neve. Your love and support mean everything to me.

—Massimo

Table of Contents

About the Author

Massimo Nardone has more than 29 years of experience in information and cybersecurity for IT/OT/IoT/IIoT, web/mobile development, cloud, and IT architecture. His true IT passions are security and Android. He holds an MSc in computing science from the University of Salerno, Italy. Throughout his working career, he has held various positions, starting as a programming developer and then security teacher, PCI QSA, auditor, assessor, lead IT/OT/SCADA/cloud architect, CISO, BISO, executive, program director, OT/IoT/IIoT security competence leader, VP of OT security, etc. In his last working engagement, he worked as a seasoned cyber and information security executive, CISO, and OT, IoT, and IIoT security competence leader, helping many clients to develop and implement cyber, information, OT, and IoT security activities. He is currently working as Vice President of OT security for SSH Communications Security. He is a author of numerous Apress books, including Secure RESTful APIs, Cybersecurity Threats & Attacks in Gaming Industry, *Pro Spring Security 6*, *Pro JPA 2 in Java EE 8*, and *Pro Android Games*, and has reviewed more than 75 titles.

About the Technical Reviewer

Naga Santhosh Reddy Vootukuri is a senior software engineering manager at Microsoft, working within the Cloud Computing + AI (C+AI) organization. With over 17 years of experience spanning across three countries (India, China, and the USA), Naga has developed a rich and varied technical background. His expertise lies in cloud computing, artificial intelligence, distributed systems, and microservices.

At Microsoft, Naga leads the Azure SQL Database team, focusing on optimizing SQL deployment processes to enhance the efficiency and scalability of services for millions of databases globally. He is responsible for the entire infrastructure of the Azure SQL deployment space and has been instrumental in the development of Master Data Services, a master data management solution by Microsoft. This project earned him recognition for delivering impactful solutions to complex data challenges.

Naga has authored and published numerous research articles in peer-reviewed and indexed journals. He is a senior member of IEEE and contributes technical articles as a Core MVB member at DZone, engaging with millions of active readers. He also serves as an editorial board member for a highly reputed science journal (*SCI*), where he reviews research articles on cloud computing and AI.

In addition to his professional roles, Naga is deeply involved in the tech community as a speaker, book reviewer for Apress, and contributor to platforms like DZone and the Microsoft Tech Community. He recently served as an IEEE AI Summit committee chair and lightning talk chair and selected some of the best lightning talks. He also delivered AI-related workshops and received an AI innovator award from Washington Senator Lisa Wellman. He also served as a judge for the Globee Awards, Fabric and AI Learning Hackathon, and Cosmos DB and AI Hackathon on devpost, which further showcased his expertise and commitment to the advancement of technology.

Acknowledgments

Many thanks go to my wonderful children Luna, Leo and Neve for your continuos support You are and will be always the most beautiful reason of my life.

I want to thank my beloved late father Giuseppe and my mother Maria, who always supported me and loved me so much. I will love and miss both of you forever.

My beloved brothers, Roberto and Mario, for your endless love and for being the best brothers in the world. Brunaldo and Kaisa for bringing joy and happiness to Luna and Leo.

Thanks a lot to Melissa Duffy for giving me the opportunity to work as writer on this book, to Sowmya Thodur for doing such a great job during the editorial process and supporting me all the time, and of course Naga Santhosh Reddy Vookuri the technical reviewer of this book, for helping me to make a better book.

—Massimo

Introduction

RESTful APIs are a common method for enabling communication between different software systems. As these Application Programming Interfaces (APIs) often handle sensitive data and critical operations, securing them is paramount. This section covers key strategies and best practices for securing RESTful APIs.

This book is for RESTful APIs beginner developers who want to learn about applying security when developing REST APIs applications. It will be a practical pocket guide and help developers understand how to develop and deploy security when dealing with RESTful APIs for authentication and authorization, data protection, threat detection and prevention, etc.

This book is a tutorial and reference that guides you through the implementation of the security features for a Java web application by presenting consistent solutions to security issues with RESTful APIs.

This book explores a comprehensive set of functionalities to implement industry-standard authentication and authorization mechanisms for Java applications, providing examples on how to develop customized RESTful APIs secure apps dealing with data validation, JSON Web Token (JWT), and Open Authorization 2.0 (OAuth 2.0).

Prerequisites

The examples in this book are all built with Java 17+ and Maven 3.9.9. Spring Security 6 was the version used throughout the book. Tomcat Web Server v11 was used for the different web applications in the book, mainly through its Maven plugin, and the laptop used was a ThinkPad Yoga 360 with 8GB of RAM. All the projects were developed using the IntelliJ IDEA Ultimate 2024.2.4.

You are free to use your own tools and operating system. Because everything is Java based, you should be able to compile your programs on any platform without problems.

Downloading the Code

The code for the examples given in this book is available via the Download Source Code button located at `https://github.com/Apress/Secure-RESTful-APIs`.

CHAPTER 1

Introduction to RESTful APIs

This chapter will explain what RESTful APIs are.

REST, which stands for Representational State Transfer, is an architectural style for designing networked applications. REST has become the predominant way of designing APIs (Application Programming Interfaces) for web-based applications.

What Are the Major Differences Between REST and SOAP?

SOAP (Simple Object Access Protocol) is a protocol for exchanging structured information in the implementation of web services. It uses XML as its message format and relies on application layer protocols like HTTP or SMTP for message negotiation and transmission. SOAP is designed to enable communication between applications running on different operating systems, with different technologies, and written in different programming languages.

REST (Representational State Transfer) and SOAP (Simple Object Access Protocol) are two different architectural styles for designing APIs.

© Massimo Nardone 2025
M. Nardone, *Secure RESTful APIs*, Apress Pocket Guides,
https://doi.org/10.1007/979-8-8688-1285-9_1

REST is more flexible and simpler, making it the preferred choice for most modern applications. SOAP, with its built-in security and transaction handling, remains valuable for enterprise-grade and mission-critical applications.

Table 1-1 shows the major differences between REST and SOAP.

Table 1-1. *Major differences between REST and SOAP*

Feature	REST	SOAP
Protocol	HTTP	HTTP, SMTP, TCP
Data format	JSON, XML	XML
Complexity	Simple	Complex
Scalability	Highly scalable	Less scalable
Performance	Faster	Slower
Use case	Web, mobile APIs	Enterprise applications

How to Combine REST and API to Create RESTful API?

An API (Application Programming Interface) is a set of rules and protocols that enable different software applications to communicate and interact with each other. It serves as a bridge between systems, allowing them to exchange data or functionality without needing to understand the details of each other's implementation.

REST APIs provide a structured and standardized way for different software applications to communicate over the Internet. They've become the backbone of modern web and mobile applications, enabling seamless integration and interaction between various services and systems.

REST APIs allow different software applications to communicate and interact with each other over the Internet using standard HTTP methods.

A RESTful API, therefore, refers to an API that is designed and implemented in compliance with the principles of REST.

Both REST and RESTful APIs are widely used for building modern web applications and services. While the terms are often used interchangeably, a RESTful API ensures full adherence to REST principles, making it a more precise implementation of the REST architecture.

HATEOAS stands for Hypermedia As The Engine Of Application State.

It is a constraint of the REST (Representational State Transfer) architectural style that enables dynamic and self-descriptive interactions in a RESTful API. With HATEOAS, clients interact with a RESTful API entirely through hyperlinks provided dynamically by the server in the responses, rather than hardcoding the API's paths and operations.

Table 1-2 describes the major differences between REST API and RESTful API.

Table 1-2. *Differences between REST API and RESTful API*

Aspect	REST API	RESTful API
Definition	Any API that uses REST principles	Strictly adheres to all REST principles
Flexibility	More flexible in design approach	Fully compliant with REST constraints
HATEOAS	May not include HATEOAS	Includes HATEOAS for navigation

What Is JSON?

JSON (JavaScript Object Notation) is a lightweight, text-based data format used for representing structured data. It is easy to read and write for humans and easy to parse and generate for machines, making it a popular choice for data exchange in web applications, APIs, and configuration files.

Here are the key features of JSON:

1. **Lightweight**: Minimal syntax and simple structure.

2. **Language Independent**: While derived from JavaScript, JSON is supported by most programming languages.

3. **Human-Readable**: Designed to be easily read and understood by humans.

4. **Versatile**: Can represent complex nested data structures like objects and arrays.

What Are the RESTful API Key Concepts?

- **Resource-Oriented**:
  - In REST, every piece of data or functionality is treated as a resource, identified by a unique URI (Uniform Resource Identifier).
  - Examples are /users, /products, and /orders.
- **Client–Server Architecture**:
  - REST separates the client (the application making the request) from the server (the application fulfilling the request), which allows them to evolve independently.
- **Stateless Communication**:
  - Each API request contains all necessary information (authentication, state, etc.).
  - The server does not store session information about clients, ensuring scalability.

- **HTTP Methods/Verbs**: RESTful APIs rely on standard HTTP methods to perform operations on resources:

  - GET

  - POST

  - PUT

  - DELETE

  - PATCH

- **Representation Formats**:

  - RESTful APIs commonly use JSON (JavaScript Object Notation) and XML to represent data.

  - JSON is preferred due to its simplicity and compatibility with modern web technologies.

- **Uniform Interface**:

  - REST enforces a standardized interface, ensuring consistent interaction between clients and servers.

What Are the HTTP Methods or Verbs?

In RESTful APIs, HTTP methods (also known as verbs) define the type of operation to perform on a given resource.

HTTP methods or verbs are fundamental to the design and operation of RESTful APIs. They provide a standardized way to perform actions on resources, ensuring clear communication between clients (e.g., web apps, mobile apps) and servers.

Each method plays a critical role in defining the behavior of a RESTful API and how it interacts with resources.

Here's a description of the commonly used HTTP methods:

- **GET**: Make a read-only request to view either a single or list of multiple resources.

- **POST**: Create a new resource based on the payload given in the body of the request.

- **DELETE**: Destroy the given resource based on the ID provided.

- **PUT**: Update the entire fields of the resource based on the given body of the request or create a new one if it does not already exist.

- **PATCH**: Partially update a resource.

What Are the HTTP Request Status Codes?

When we receive an HTTP request in the basic RESTful format, the server will return an HTTP status code and any optional JSON payloads.

The most common HTTP status codes are listed in Table 1-3.

Table 1-3. *The most common HTTP status codes*

Status code	Meaning
200 OK	Request is successful.
301 Moved Permanently	Page has been moved.
401 Unauthorized	Server requires authentication.
403 Forbidden	Client authenticated but no permissions to view resource.
404 Not Found	Page not found.
500 Internal Server Error	Server-side error.
503 Server Unavailable	Server-side error.

Problem

Why use RESTful APIs?

Solution

RESTful APIs are used generally for the following reasons:

1. **Platform Independence**:

   - RESTful APIs can be consumed by any client (web, mobile, IoT) capable of making HTTP requests.

2. **Scalability**:

   - Statelessness and simplicity make RESTful APIs ideal for handling a large number of requests.

3. **Ease of Integration**:

   - They enable seamless communication between different systems and technologies.

4. **Flexibility:**

- Clients can request only the data they need, optimizing bandwidth and improving performance.

5. **Widely Adopted:**

- Supported by most programming languages and frameworks, making them a go-to choice for API development.

Problem

What are the RESTful APIs Core Components?

Solution

Core Components of RESTful APIs include the following:

1. **Endpoints:**

- URLs that represent resources, e.g., `https://api.example.com/users`.

2. **HTTP Methods:**

- Specify the action to perform on a resource.

3. **Headers:**

- Provide metadata for requests and responses (e.g., authentication tokens, content types).

4. **Request Body:**

- Contains data for POST, PUT, or PATCH requests (usually in JSON or XML format).

5. **Response Body**:

   - Contains the server's response, often including data or status messages.

6. **Status Codes**:

   - HTTP status codes inform clients of the result of their request (as explained previously).

Problem

What are the most common advantages and disadvantages of RESTful APIs?

Solution

Here are the most important advantages of RESTful APIs:

- **Scalability**: RESTful architectures are scalable due to their stateless nature.

- **Flexibility**: Clients and servers can evolve independently without affecting each other as long as the API contract remains consistent.

- **Wide Adoption**: REST is widely adopted and understood, making it easier for developers to work with.

- **Caching**: REST APIs can take advantage of HTTP caching mechanisms to improve performance.

- **Language and Platform Independence**: Since REST APIs use standard HTTP methods and formats, they can be accessed from various programming languages and platforms.

While REST APIs have numerous advantages, there are also some disadvantages and limitations to consider:

- **Lack of Standardization**: Despite being a widely adopted architectural style, REST doesn't provide strict guidelines on how to design APIs. This can lead to inconsistencies in API design and make it challenging to ensure uniformity across different APIs.

- **Overfetching and Underfetching**: REST APIs often return fixed data structures, which can lead to overfetching (receiving more data than needed) or underfetching (receiving less data than needed) of information. This can result in wasted bandwidth or additional requests.

- **Limited Support for Real-Time Communication**: REST APIs are typically request–response-based and may not be well-suited for real-time communication. Implementing features like instant messaging or live updates can be complex and might require additional technologies.

- **No Built-In State Management**: REST APIs are stateless, which means the server doesn't store client state. While this simplifies server design, it can lead to challenges when managing session-related information.

- **Lack of Rich Semantics**: REST APIs primarily rely on HTTP methods and status codes, which may not always convey rich semantics about the underlying operations. This can lead to ambiguity in understanding the purpose of certain API endpoints.

- **Performance Overhead**: REST APIs may involve additional data parsing and serialization steps due to their reliance on formats like JSON or XML. This can introduce performance overhead, especially in high-frequency scenarios.

- **Multiple Requests for Complex Operations**: Complex operations often require multiple requests to the server, leading to additional network overhead and latency. This can be a concern for mobile applications or in situations with limited bandwidth.

- **Lack of Flexibility in Versioning**: Making changes to a REST API while maintaining backward compatibility can be challenging. Different versions of the API might need to be managed, which can complicate the development and deployment process.

- **Security Considerations**: While REST APIs can be secured using mechanisms like HTTPS and authentication, designing a secure REST API requires careful consideration of authorization, token management, and protection against common security vulnerabilities.

- **Limited Discoverability**: Discovering the available endpoints and their functionalities in a REST API might require external documentation, as there's no built-in mechanism for exposing the API structure to clients.

Finally, here is a simple example of a simple RESTful API for managing a list of cars:

- GET /cars: Retrieve a list of all cars.

- GET /cars/{id}: Retrieve details of a specific car.

- POST /cars: Create a new car record by sending car data.

- PUT /cars/{id}: Update details of a specific car.

- DELETE /cars/{id}: Delete a specific car.

Here is how a request (GET car information) HTTP looks like:

GET https://api.example.com/cars/123

Headers:

```
Authorization: Bearer <token>
```

Response JSON:

```
{
    car_id: 123,
    name": "Ferrari",
    response_id: 1
}
```

A RESTful API flow example is shown in Figure 1-1.

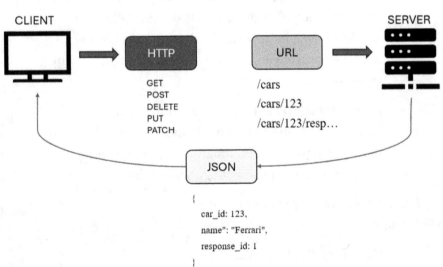

Figure 1-1. *RESTful example process flow*

Summary

RESTful APIs provide a standardized, efficient, and flexible approach to building modern web services. They are designed to simplify data exchange between clients and servers while supporting scalability and maintainability, making them a cornerstone of modern software development.

In this chapter, we first introduced REST, APIs, SOAP, JSON, and how to combine some of these to get RESTful APIs. We explained the REST API key concepts, the advantages, disadvantages, and limitations to consider for REST APIs and finally provided a simple example of a RESTful API.

CHAPTER 2

Key Security Concerns and Risks for RESTful APIs

This chapter will explain what the most common key security concerns and risks for RESTful APIs are.

RESTful APIs are a backbone of modern web and mobile applications, enabling seamless communication between clients and servers. However, as APIs expose sensitive data and critical application functionality, they become prime targets for attackers. Understanding the key security concerns and risks is essential to building secure and reliable RESTful APIs.

What Are the RESTful API Key Security Concerns?

Here are key security concerns for RESTful APIs:

1. **Authentication and Authorization**:

    - Ensuring that only legitimate users or systems can access API resources.

    - Risks include weak authentication mechanisms and unauthorized access to sensitive data.

© Massimo Nardone 2025
M. Nardone, *Secure RESTful APIs*, Apress Pocket Guides,
https://doi.org/10.1007/979-8-8688-1285-9_2

2. **Data Exposure**:

- APIs often transmit sensitive data such as personal information or financial details.

- Improper handling or lack of encryption can lead to data leaks.

3. **Lack of Input Validation**:

- APIs may accept malicious or improperly formatted input, leading to injection attacks like SQL injection or XML external entities (XXEs).

4. **Rate Limiting and Throttling**:

- Without rate limiting, APIs can be overwhelmed by excessive requests (denial-of-service (DoS)/ distributed DoS (DDoS) attacks).

- Overexposed APIs can unintentionally allow data scraping.

5. **Data Integrity**:

- Ensuring that data sent and received by the API is not tampered with during transmission.

- Risks include man-in-the-middle (MITM) attacks.

6. **Improper Error Handling**:

- Revealing sensitive system information in error messages can give attackers insight into the API's structure.

7. **Session Management**:

- Weak session handling mechanisms can lead to session hijacking or fixation attacks.

8. **CORS (Cross-Origin Resource Sharing) Misconfiguration**:

    - Improperly configured CORS policies can allow malicious sites to access API data.

9. **Token and Credential Exposure**:

    - Storing API keys, tokens, or credentials insecurely can lead to unauthorized access.

10. **API Versioning and Deprecation Risks**:

    - Unsecured older versions of APIs remain vulnerable to attacks if not deprecated or maintained properly.

What Are the Most Common Sources of Risk?

In general, the most common sources of risk are

- **Poor Authentication**: Weak or missing authentication mechanisms allow unauthorized access.

- **Insufficient Input Validation**: Lack of validation leads to injection attacks and data manipulation.

- **Excessive Data Exposure**: APIs that return more information than necessary can inadvertently leak sensitive data.

- **Rate Limiting Neglect**: APIs without rate limiting are vulnerable to denial-of-service (DoS) attacks.

- **Outdated Dependencies**: Using insecure libraries or frameworks introduces vulnerabilities.

What Are the Common Risks Associated with RESTful APIs?

1. **Lack of Authentication and Authorization**

   - **Risk**: APIs without proper authentication and authorization controls may allow unauthorized users to access sensitive data or perform restricted actions.

   - **Example**: A public-facing API endpoint without user authentication might expose user data or allow account hijacking.

2. **Insufficient Encryption**

   - **Risk**: Failure to encrypt data in transit (e.g., over HTTP instead of HTTPS) exposes sensitive information to interception (man-in-the-middle attacks).

   - **Example**: Sending sensitive data like API keys or credentials over an unencrypted channel.

3. **Exposure of Sensitive Data**

   - **Risk**: APIs may inadvertently expose sensitive information in responses, such as passwords, personal data, or API keys.

   - **Example**: Error messages returning stack traces or database query information.

4. **Injection Attacks**

   - **Risk**: APIs that fail to validate or sanitize user inputs are vulnerable to injection attacks, such as SQL injection or script injection.

- **Example**: An attacker injects malicious code through query parameters or payloads.

5. **Rate Limiting and DDoS Vulnerabilities**

   - **Risk**: Lack of rate limiting allows attackers to overload an API with requests, leading to denial-of-service attacks or resource exhaustion.

   - **Example**: An attacker sends thousands of requests per second, causing API unavailability.

6. **Broken Object-Level Authorization**

   - **Risk**: APIs that fail to enforce proper access control policies at the object level may allow users to access data they do not own.

   - **Example**: An attacker guesses object identifiers (e.g., userId) and accesses another user's data.

7. **API Parameter Tampering**

   - **Risk**: Manipulation of API parameters, such as query strings, headers, or cookies, to exploit vulnerabilities.

   - **Example**: Changing a userRole parameter to gain admin privileges.

8. **Misconfigured CORS (Cross-Origin Resource Sharing)**

   - **Risk**: APIs with overly permissive CORS configurations allow unauthorized domains to access resources.

   - **Example**: An attacker's malicious domain accesses sensitive data from an API.

9. **Insufficient Logging and Monitoring**

    - **Risk**: Failure to log and monitor API activities leads to delayed detection of malicious activities.

    - **Example**: Missing alerts for unusual activity patterns, like brute-force login attempts.

10. **Lack of Input Validation**

    - **Risk**: APIs that do not validate input can be exploited for buffer overflows, path traversal, or other vulnerabilities.

    - **Example**: An attacker uploads malicious files by bypassing file validation.

11. **Insecure API Key Management**

    - **Risk**: Hardcoding API keys or failing to rotate them periodically can lead to unauthorized use.

    - **Example**: An attacker gains access to an API key through public repositories or shared credentials.

12. **Third-Party Dependencies**

    - **Risk**: Using insecure third-party APIs or libraries in the application stack can introduce vulnerabilities.

    - **Example**: A third-party API is compromised and serves malicious payloads.

What Are the Most Common RESTful APIs Risk Mitigation Strategies?

RESTful APIs risk mitigation strategies include

1. **Authentication and Authorization**: Use secure protocols like OAuth2 and enforce role-based access control (RBAC).

2. **Encryption**: Implement HTTPS and encrypt sensitive data in transit.

3. **Data Minimization**: Only return necessary data in API responses.

4. **Input Validation**: Validate and sanitize all user inputs to prevent injection attacks.

5. **Rate Limiting**: Implement rate limiting and throttling to prevent abuse.

6. **Object-Level Security**: Ensure strict access control at the object level.

7. **CORS Configuration**: Limit allowed origins and enforce strict CORS policies.

8. **Secure API Key Management**: Rotate keys periodically and avoid hardcoding them.

9. **Comprehensive Logging**: Monitor API traffic and set up alerts for unusual activities.

10. **Security Testing**: Conduct regular vulnerability assessments and penetration testing.

11. **Error Handling**: Avoid exposing detailed error messages that could provide attackers with insights into your API structure or vulnerabilities.

12. **API Gateway Security**: Use API gateway to centralize security controls like authentication, rate limiting, and request filtering. Implement Web Application Firewalls (WAF) rules to detect and block malicious traffic.

13. **Versioning and Deprecation Policy**: Outlines how an organization manages changes to its software, APIs, or services over time.

14. **Schema Validation**: Define and enforce a strict schema for request payloads.

15. **Security Headers**: Use headers like strict-transport-security and x-frame-options to enhance security.

By addressing these risks proactively, organizations can significantly enhance the security of their RESTful APIs, safeguarding sensitive data and maintaining trust with users and partners.

Summary

RESTful APIs are vital for modern applications but come with inherent security challenges. Addressing these concerns through robust security measures, best practices, and continuous monitoring is essential to protect both the API and its consumers from potential threats. By understanding and mitigating these risks, developers can build APIs that are not only functional but also resilient against evolving cyber threats.

In this chapter, we introduced what the most common key security concerns and risks for RESTful APIs are and how to mitigate them.

CHAPTER 3

Data Protection and Validation for RESTful APIs

This chapter will explain data protection and validation for RESTful APIs.

What Is Data Protection?

Data protection refers to the practices, policies, and technologies implemented to safeguard sensitive, personal, and organizational data from unauthorized access, misuse, theft, or corruption. It ensures the confidentiality, integrity, and availability of data throughout its life cycle, whether in transit, at rest, or in use.

1. What Are the Main Key Objectives of Data Protection?

The key objectives of data protection are

1. **Confidentiality**: Ensures that only authorized individuals or systems can access sensitive information

© Massimo Nardone 2025
M. Nardone, *Secure RESTful APIs*, Apress Pocket Guides,
https://doi.org/10.1007/979-8-8688-1285-9_3

2. **Integrity**: Maintains the accuracy and completeness of data, preventing unauthorized modification

3. **Availability**: Ensures that data is accessible to authorized users whenever it is needed

2. Why Is Data Protection Important?

Data protection is crucial for several reasons, including legal, financial, ethical, and security considerations:

- **Compliance**: Helps organizations adhere to legal regulations like GDPR, CCPA, and HIPAA

- **Trust**: Builds trust with customers by safeguarding their personal information

- **Security**: Protects against cyber threats like data breaches, ransomware, and insider threats

- **Business Continuity**: Ensures uninterrupted operations by protecting critical data from loss or damage

3. What Are the Most Common Data Protection Practices?

Implementing robust data protection measures ensures the security, confidentiality, and integrity of sensitive information.

Here are the common practices organizations and individuals can adopt to protect data:

1. **Encryption**: Securing data by converting it into a coded format that is unreadable without a key

2. **Access Controls**: Restricting access to data based on roles, permissions, and authentication

3. **Data Masking**: Hiding sensitive data by replacing it with fictitious data while maintaining usability

4. **Backup and Recovery**: Regularly copying data to ensure it can be restored in case of loss or corruption

5. **Data Minimization**: Collecting and retaining only the data necessary for specific purposes

6. **Auditing and Monitoring**: Continuously monitoring data access and usage to detect anomalies

These practices, when implemented effectively, form a comprehensive strategy for protecting sensitive data against threats, ensuring compliance, and maintaining trust. Data protection is an ongoing process that requires continuous monitoring, updates, and education.

4. What Are the Most Important Types of Data Protection?

Data protection encompasses a range of techniques and strategies to ensure the security, integrity, and privacy of sensitive data.

Here are the most important types of data protection:

1. **Physical Data Protection:**

   • Securing physical access to servers, storage devices, and backups

2. **Digital Data Protection:**

   • Using firewalls, antivirus software, and encryption to protect data in digital systems

3. **Cloud Data Protection:**

- Implementing security measures for data stored in cloud environments, such as access controls and encryption

4. **Compliance-Based Protection:**

- Meeting the requirements of data protection laws and standards

Each type of data protection plays a unique role in securing sensitive information. A comprehensive data protection strategy often involves combining these types to address different threats and vulnerabilities, ensuring robust security across all aspects of data handling and storage.

RESTful API Data Security

Data security for RESTful APIs involves implementing measures to protect sensitive information exchanged between clients and servers. APIs are vulnerable to threats like data breaches, interception, unauthorized access, and injection attacks, making robust security practices essential.

Securing RESTful APIs is essential for safeguarding sensitive data and maintaining trust. By following these practices, developers can mitigate risks, ensure data privacy, and protect against unauthorized access or attacks.

5. What Are the Key Principles for RESTful API Data Security?

Securing RESTful APIs is critical to protect sensitive data, ensure user privacy, and maintain the integrity of communication.

The most important principles for RESTful API Data Security are

1. **Authentication**: Verifying the identity of users or systems accessing the API

2. **Authorization**: Ensuring users or systems can only access resources they are permitted to

3. **Data Integrity**: Preventing unauthorized data modification during transmission

4. **Confidentiality**: Securing sensitive information from unauthorized access

5. **Non-repudiation**: Providing evidence of actions performed within the API system

Let's elaborate the key principles for RESTful API Data Security:

1. **Use HTTPS**

   - **Purpose**: Encrypts data in transit to prevent interception.

   - **Implementation**:

     - Always enforce HTTPS to secure communication between clients and servers.

     - Use certificates from trusted Certificate Authorities (CAs).

2. **Authentication**

   - **Purpose**: Verifies the identity of users accessing the API.

   - **Methods**:

     - **Token-Based Authentication**:

       - Use JSON Web Token (JWT) or OAuth 2.0 tokens for stateless authentication.

- **API Keys:**

  - Assign unique keys to each client for identification.

- **Multi-factor Authentication (MFA):**

  - Add an extra layer of security for sensitive APIs.

3. **Authorization**

- **Purpose**: Ensures users have appropriate permissions to access resources.

- **Best Practices**:

  - Use role-based access control (RBAC) or attribute-based access control (ABAC).

  - Enforce least privilege access principles.

4. **Input Validation and Sanitization**

- **Purpose**: Prevents injection attacks like SQL injection or XSS.

- **Best Practices**:

  - Validate all user inputs against predefined schemas.

  - Sanitize inputs to remove potentially malicious code.

  - Use libraries like OWASP's ESAPI for secure input handling.

5. **Rate Limiting and Throttling**

   - **Purpose**: Protects APIs from abuse, such as DDoS attacks.

   - **Implementation**:

     - Set limits on the number of requests per client/ IP within a specified time frame.

     - Use tools like API gateways or rate-limiting middleware.

6. **Secure Data Storage**

   - **Purpose**: Protects sensitive data at rest.

   - **Best Practices**:

     - Encrypt sensitive data using algorithms like AES-256.

     - Avoid storing sensitive information in log files or plain text.

     - Implement database security measures, such as access restrictions.

7. **Token Expiration and Revocation**

   - **Purpose**: Reduces the risk of token misuse.

   - **Best Practices**:

     - Use short-lived tokens to minimize the impact of a stolen token.

     - Provide refresh tokens for reauthentication.

     - Implement token revocation mechanisms to invalidate compromised tokens.

8. **Error Handling and Logging**

   - **Purpose**: Prevents leakage of sensitive information through errors.

   - **Best Practices**:

     - Avoid detailed error messages that expose server details.

     - Use generic error messages (e.g., "Unauthorized" or "Bad Request").

     - Log errors securely for monitoring and debugging purposes.

9. **Content Security**

   - **Purpose**: Prevents attacks like JSON hijacking or XML external entity (XXE) attacks.

   - **Best Practices**:

     - Use appropriate content types and headers (e.g., Content-Type: application/json).

     - Disable XML parsing if not needed or secure it against XXE attacks.

10. **API Gateway and Firewall**

    - **Purpose**: Acts as an intermediary to enhance security.

    - **Implementation**:

      - Use API gateways for request filtering, rate limiting, and authentication.

      - Employ Web Application Firewalls (WAF) to block malicious traffic.

11. **Secure Cross-Origin Resource Sharing (CORS)**

- **Purpose**: Manages how resources are shared between different origins.

- **Best Practices**:

  - Restrict CORS policies to trusted origins only.

  - Use appropriate HTTP methods in CORS headers (e.g., GET, POST).

12. **Security Headers**

- **Purpose**: Adds additional layers of protection.

- **Examples**:

  - **Content Security Policy (CSP)**: Mitigates XSS attacks.

  - **X-Frame-Options**: Prevents clickjacking.

  - **Strict-Transport-Security (HSTS)**: Enforces HTTPS usage.

13. **Regular Security Audits and Updates**

- **Purpose**: Identifies and mitigates vulnerabilities.

- **Best Practices**:

  - Conduct penetration testing and vulnerability assessments regularly.

  - Keep API dependencies and libraries up to date.

14. **Data Minimization**

   - **Purpose**: Reduces risk by limiting exposed data.

   - **Best Practices**:

      - Only return the necessary data in API responses (e.g., avoid overfetching).

      - Mask or anonymize sensitive data before sharing.

15. **Use OAuth 2.0 for Authorization**

   - **Purpose**: Provides a robust framework for access delegation.

   - **Features**:

      - Supports token-based authentication for secure access.

      - Integrates with identity providers like Google, GitHub, or Okta.

16. **Logging and Monitoring**

   - **Purpose**: Detects and responds to suspicious activities.

   - **Best Practices**:

      - Log all API requests and responses securely.

      - Monitor API usage patterns for anomalies.

17. **Secure API Documentation**

   - **Purpose**: Prevents unintentional exposure of sensitive details.

- **Best Practices**:

  - Limit access to API documentation to authenticated users.

  - Avoid publishing sensitive data like API keys or credentials.

By following these principles, you can build robust and secure RESTful APIs that protect sensitive data, ensure compliance with regulations, and maintain user trust.

6. What Does RESTful API Security Look Like?

Here are practical examples showcasing different security techniques to protect RESTful APIs:

1. **HTTPS Implementation**

   Ensure all API traffic is encrypted.

   Example with Spring Boot:

   ```
   server:
     ssl:
       key-store: classpath:keystore.jks
       key-store-password: password
       key-alias: tomcat
       enabled: true
   ```

   - This config enforces HTTPS by providing an SSL certificate (keystore.jks).

2. **Authentication with JWT**

Use JSON Web Token for stateless authentication.

Steps:

1. **Login Endpoint**: Generate a JWT upon successful login.

2. **Verify Token**: Validate the token on each request.

Example Login Endpoint (Spring Boot):

```
@PostMapping("/login")
public ResponseEntity<?> authenticateUser(@RequestBody
LoginRequest loginRequest) {
    String token = jwtUtils.generateToken(loginRequest.
    getUsername());
    return ResponseEntity.ok(new JwtResponse(token));
}
```

Securing Endpoints (Java Example):

```
@EnableWebSecurity
public class SecurityConfig extends
WebSecurityConfigurerAdapter {
    @Override
    protected void configure(HttpSecurity http) throws
    Exception {
        http.csrf().disable()
            .authorizeRequests()
            .antMatchers("/login").permitAll()
            .anyRequest().authenticated()
            .and()
            .addFilter(new JwtAuthenticationFilter
            (authenticationManager()));
    }
}
```

3. **Role-Based Access Control**

   Restrict access to endpoints based on user roles.

   Java Example:

```
@PreAuthorize("hasRole('ADMIN')")
@GetMapping("/admin")
public String adminOnlyEndpoint() {
    return "Admin Access Granted!";
}
```

   - Only users with the ADMIN role can access this
     endpoint.

4. **Input Validation and Sanitization**

   Prevent injection attacks by validating API inputs.

   Java Example Using Hibernate Validator:

```
public class UserRequest {
    @NotNull
    @Size(min = 3, max = 20)
    private String username;

    @Email
    private String email;
}
```

   Validation in Controller Java Example:

```
@PostMapping("/register")
public ResponseEntity<?> registerUser(@Valid
@RequestBody UserRequest userRequest) {
    // Logic here
}
```

5. **Rate Limiting with API Gateway**

Limit the number of requests a client can make.

Example with Spring Boot:

```java
@Bean
public RouteLocator rateLimitRoutes(RouteLocatorBuilder
builder) {
    return builder.routes()
        .route("limit_route", r -> r.path("/api/**")
            .filters(f -> f.requestRateLimiter(c ->
            c.setRateLimiter(redisRateLimiter())))
            .uri("http://localhost:8080"))
        .build();
}
```

6. **OAuth 2.0 Authorization**

Secure APIs using third-party identity providers
(e.g., Google, GitHub).

Java Example (Spring Security OAuth2):

```java
@EnableWebSecurity
public class OAuth2SecurityConfig extends
WebSecurityConfigurerAdapter {
    @Override
    protected void configure(HttpSecurity http) throws
    Exception {
        http.oauth2Login()
            .loginPage("/login")
            .defaultSuccessURL("/home", true);
    }
}
```

Configuration for Google:

```
spring:
  security:
    oauth2:
      client:
        registration:
          google:
            client-id: your-google-client-id
            client-secret: your-google-client-secret
            redirect-uri: "{baseUrl}/login/oauth2/
            code/google"
```

7. **API Key Authentication**

   Restrict access using API keys.

   Example with Middleware:

```
public class ApiKeyFilter extends OncePerRequestFilter {
    @Override
    protected void doFilterInternal(HttpServlet
    Request request, HttpServletResponse response,
    FilterChain chain)
            throws ServletException, IOException {
        String apiKey = request.getHeader("X-API-KEY");
        if (!"valid-api-key".equals(apiKey)) {
            response.setStatus(HttpServletResponse.
            SC_UNAUTHORIZED);
            return;
        }
        chain.doFilter(request, response);
    }
}
```

Add Filter to Security Config:

```
@Override
protected void configure(HttpSecurity http) throws
Exception {
    http.addFilterBefore(new
ApiKeyFilter(),
UsernamePasswordAuthenticationFilter.class);
}
```

8. **Content Security**

Protect API responses against injection attacks.

Java Example:

```
@GetMapping("/user")
public ResponseEntity<?> getUser() {
    HttpHeaders headers = new HttpHeaders();
    headers.add("Content-Security-Policy",
    "default-src 'self'");
    return ResponseEntity.ok().headers(headers).
    body("User Data");
}
```

9. **Hiding Sensitive Information**

Mask or exclude sensitive data in API responses.

Example with Jackson (Masking Sensitive Data):

```
@JsonProperty(access = JsonProperty.Access.WRITE_ONLY)
private String password;
```

- The password will not be included in API responses.

10. **Logging and Monitoring**

Capture activity logs for security analysis.

Example Using SLF4J:

```
private static final Logger logger = LoggerFactory.
getLogger(UserController.class);

@GetMapping("/users")
public ResponseEntity<?> getUsers() {
    logger.info("Fetching all users");
    return ResponseEntity.ok(userService.
    getAllUsers());
}
```

Implementing these examples ensures a comprehensive security layer for your RESTful API. By combining HTTPS, authentication, rate limiting, and input validation, you can protect sensitive data and prevent unauthorized access effectively.

Why Do Data Validation for RESTful APIs and How?

Data validation for RESTful APIs ensures that the data provided by the client meets the API's expectations. Proper validation enhances security, maintains data integrity, and provides clear error responses.

Data validation is generally performed for the following reasons:

- Prevent invalid data from entering your system.

- Protect against injection attacks and other vulnerabilities.

- Ensure compliance with business rules and data formats.

- Enhance the user experience by providing meaningful error messages.

Problem

What are the most common types of data validation?

Solution

The most common types of data validation include

- **Data Type Validation**

  Verify the data matches expected types, e.g., strings, integers, or Booleans.

- **Range Validation**

  Ensure numbers or dates fall within acceptable ranges.

- **Format Validation**

  Validate email addresses, phone numbers, and other formatted fields using patterns or regular expressions (REGEX).

- **Length Validation**

  Limit the size of strings or arrays to prevent performance issues.

- **Custom Business Logic Validation**

  Apply rules specific to your application, e.g., checking if a username is unique.

7. How to Perform Data Validation in RESTful APIs?

Here is how generally data validation is performed:

- **Server-Side Validation**

    - Always validate data on the server to ensure security, even if client-side validation is in place.

- **Client-Side Validation (Optional)**

    - Provides a better user experience but should never replace server-side validation.

Here is a full example of data validation in RESTful APIs. Validation steps in Spring Boot (Java) include the following:

1. **Add Validation Dependency**:

```
<dependency>
    <groupId>org.springframework.boot</groupId>
    <artifactId>spring-boot-starter-validation
    </artifactId>
</dependency>
```

2. **Define a DTO with Validation Annotations**:

```
import jakarta.validation.constraints.*;

public class UserRequest {
    @NotNull
    @Size(min = 3, max = 50)
    private String username;
```

```
@Email
private String email;

@Pattern(regexp = "^[0-9]{10}$", message = "Phone
number must be 10 digits")
private String phoneNumber;

@Min(18)
@Max(100)
private int age;
}
```

3. **Apply Validation in the Controller**:

```
@RestController
@RequestMapping("/users")
public class UserController {
    @PostMapping("/register")
    public ResponseEntity<String> registerUser(@Valid
    @RequestBody UserRequest userRequest) {
        return ResponseEntity.ok("User registered
        successfully");
    }
}
```

4. **Handle Validation Errors**: Spring Boot automatically handles validation errors and returns HTTP 400 with details.

Summary

In this chapter, we described data protection and validation for RESTful APIs. We started introducing the main key objectives of data protection and why in general data protection is so important.

We elaborated the key principles for RESTful API Data Security and the best practices to consider.

Finally, we provided a good set of examples showcasing different security techniques to protect RESTful APIs including HTTPS, JWT, etc.

CHAPTER 4

JSON Web Token (JWT) Authentication

This chapter will explore REST API and JSON Web Token (JWT) authentication and authorization using Spring Boot 3, Spring Security 6, and PostgreSQL DB.

What Is JSON Web Token (JWT)?

JSON Web Token (JWT) is an open standard (RFC 7519) that defines a compact and self-contained way for securely transmitting information between parties as a JSON object. JWTs are commonly used for authentication and authorization purposes in web applications and APIs.

A JWT consists of three parts:

1. **Header**: The header typically consists of two parts—the type of the token (JWT) and the signing algorithm being used, such as HMAC SHA256 or RSA.

   ```
   {
     "alg": "HS256",
     "typ": "JWT"
   }
   ```

© Massimo Nardone 2025
M. Nardone, *Secure RESTful APIs*, Apress Pocket Guides,
https://doi.org/10.1007/979-8-8688-1285-9_4

2. **Payload**: The second part of the token is the payload, which contains the claims. Claims are statements about an entity (typically the user) and additional metadata and can be categorized into three types:

- **Registered Claims**: These are predefined claims with specific meanings, like iss (issuer), exp (expiration time), sub (subject), and more.

- **Public Claims**: These are custom claims that you define to convey additional information.

- **Private Claims**: These are custom claims that are meant to be shared between parties that agree on their usage and are not defined in any public specification.

```
{
  "sub": "1234567890",
  "name": "Massimo Nardone",
  "iat": 6723561290
}
```

3. **Signature**: To create the signature part, you have to take the encoded header, the encoded payload, a secret, and the algorithm specified in the header and sign that. The signature is used to verify that the sender of the JWT is who it says it is and to ensure that the message wasn't changed along the way.

Here is how JWTs work:

- **Authentication**: When a user logs in, the server creates a JWT containing the user's information and signs it with a secret key. This JWT is then sent to the client.

- **Authorization**: The client includes the JWT in the headers of subsequent requests to the server. The server can then verify the JWT's signature and extract the user's information from the payload to grant access to protected resources.

Figure 4-1 shows how JWT works.

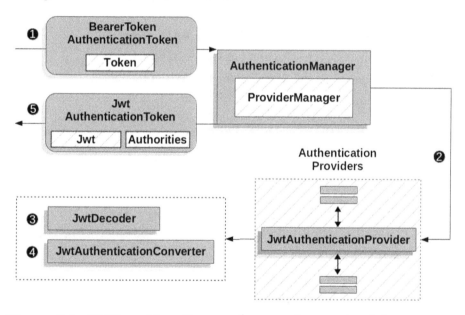

Figure 4-1. *JWT working diagram (source: docs.spring.io)*

1. The authentication filter dissects the following process: First, the bearer token passes a BearerTokenAuthenticationToken to the AuthenticationManager, which is implemented by the ProviderManager.

2. The ProviderManager is configured to use an AuthenticationProvider of type JwtAuthenticationProvider.

3. JwtAuthenticationProvider decodes, verifies, and validates the Jwt using a JwtDecoder.

4. JwtAuthenticationProvider then uses the JwtAuthenticationConverter to convert the Jwt into a collection of granted authorities.

5. When authentication is successful, the authentication that is returned is of type JwtAuthenticationToken and has a principal that is the Jwt returned by the configured JwtDecoder. Ultimately, the returned JwtAuthenticationToken will be set on the SecurityContextHolder by the authentication filter.

The advantages of JWT are as follows:

- **Compact**: JWTs are compact and can be sent as URL parameters, in an HTTP header, or in cookies.

- **Self-Contained**: The token itself contains all the necessary information, reducing the need to query a database for user information.

- **Decentralized**: Since JWTs are self-contained, the server doesn't need to keep session information, making it easier to scale and distribute applications.

For security purposes, JWTs are digitally signed rather than encrypted. While the token's contents can be decoded by anyone with access, the signature ensures its integrity. Sensitive data should not be stored in the payload, as it can be easily decoded.

To prevent tampering, it's crucial to use robust and secure algorithms for signing tokens. Signing secrets must be kept confidential, and if public-key cryptography is used, the private key must remain secure.

JWTs are commonly used to implement secure authentication and authorization mechanisms in modern web applications, APIs, and single sign-on (SSO) systems.

We can now start to build an example to show how to secure a REST API using JSON Web Token (JWT) using Spring Security v6, Spring Boot v3+, and PostgreSQL DB.

As the first step, let's download and install PostgreSQL from `https://www.postgresql.org/download/windows/`.

1. How Do We Create a New DB and User in PostgreSQL?

To create a new DB named "jwtsecuritydb" with username = postgres and password = postgres, use the following commands:

```
postgres=# create database jwtsecuritydb;
postgres=# create user postgres with encrypted password
'postgres';
postgres=# grant all privileges on database jwtsecuritydb to
postgres;
```

Figure 4-2 shows that our new PostgreSQL DB is up and running.

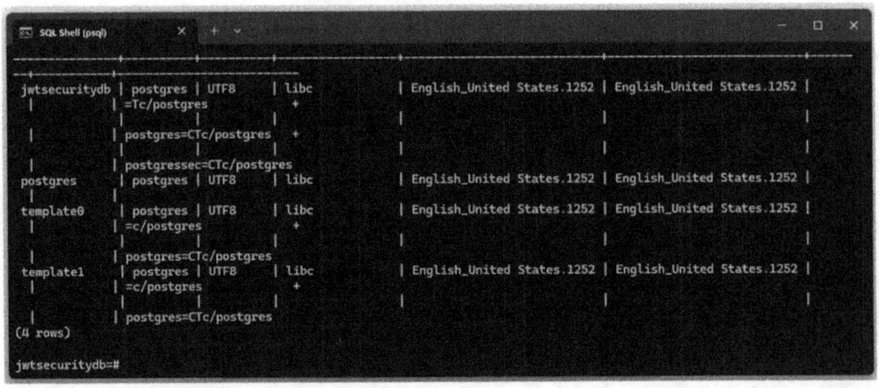

Figure 4-2. *PostgreSQL shell console*

2. How Do We Create a New Project with Spring Initializr?

Let's create a new Spring project named JWT_Security_Authentication using the Spring Initializr web tool at `https://start.spring.io/` as shown in Figure 4-3.

Figure 4-3. *New Spring project using Spring Initializr*

For our example we chose Java 23, Maven, JAR, Spring Web, PostgreSQL Driver, Spring Security, Spring Data JPA, and Lombok as dependencies.

The project's file structure is shown in Figure 4-4.

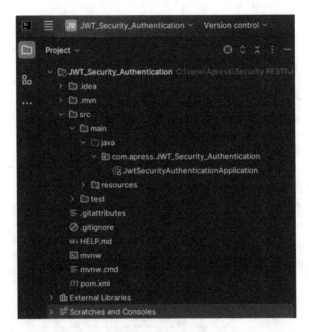

Figure 4-4. *New Spring project structure*

Next, we will add the needed dependencies in POM.xml files such as JSON Web Token "io.jsonwebtoken" and Jakarta XML Binding "jaxb-api." The entire POM.xml file is showed in **Listing 4-1**.

Listing 4-1. The POM.xml file

```
<?xml version="1.0" encoding="UTF-8"?>
<project xmlns="http://maven.apache.org/POM/4.0.0"
xmlns:xsi="http://www.w3.org/2001/XMLSchema-instance"
        xsi:schemaLocation="http://maven.apache.org/POM/4.0.0
        https://maven.apache.org/xsd/maven-4.0.0.xsd">
    <modelVersion>4.0.0</modelVersion>
```

```
<parent>
    <groupId>org.springframework.boot</groupId>
    <artifactId>spring-boot-starter-parent</artifactId>
    <version>3.3.5</version>
    <relativePath/> <!-- lookup parent from repository -->
</parent>
<groupId>com.apress</groupId>
<artifactId>JWT_Security_Authentication</artifactId>
<version>0.0.1-SNAPSHOT</version>
<name>JWT_Security_Authentication</name>
<description>Demo project for Spring Boot</description>
<url/>
<licenses>
    <license/>
</licenses>
<developers>
    <developer/>
</developers>
<scm>
    <connection/>
    <developerConnection/>
    <tag/>
    <url/>
</scm>
<properties>
    <java.version>23</java.version>
</properties>
<dependencies>
    <dependency>
        <groupId>org.springframework.boot</groupId>
        <artifactId>spring-boot-starter-data-jpa</artifactId>
    </dependency>
```

```xml
<dependency>
    <groupId>org.springframework.boot</groupId>
    <artifactId>spring-boot-starter-security</artifactId>
</dependency>
<dependency>
    <groupId>org.springframework.boot</groupId>
    <artifactId>spring-boot-starter-web</artifactId>
</dependency>

<dependency>
    <groupId>org.postgresql</groupId>
    <artifactId>postgresql</artifactId>
    <scope>runtime</scope>
</dependency>
<dependency>
    <groupId>org.projectlombok</groupId>
    <artifactId>lombok</artifactId>
    <optional>true</optional>
</dependency>
<dependency>
    <groupId>org.springframework.boot</groupId>
    <artifactId>spring-boot-starter-test</artifactId>
    <scope>test</scope>
</dependency>
<dependency>
    <groupId>org.springframework.security</groupId>
    <artifactId>spring-security-test</artifactId>
    <scope>test</scope>
</dependency>
```

```xml
<dependency>
    <groupId>io.jsonwebtoken</groupId>
    <artifactId>jjwt</artifactId>
    <version>0.9.1</version>
</dependency>

<!-- JAXB API -->
<dependency>
    <groupId>javax.xml.bind</groupId>
    <artifactId>jaxb-api</artifactId>
    <version>2.3.1</version>
</dependency>

<!-- JAXB Core Implementation -->
<dependency>
    <groupId>org.glassfish.jaxb</groupId>
    <artifactId>jaxb-runtime</artifactId>
    <version>2.3.1</version>
</dependency>

</dependencies>

<build>
    <plugins>
        <plugin>
            <groupId>org.springframework.boot</groupId>
            <artifactId>spring-boot-maven-plugin</artifactId>
            <configuration>
                <excludes>
                    <exclude>
                        <groupId>org.projectlombok</groupId>
                        <artifactId>lombok</artifactId>
                    </exclude>
```

```
        </excludes>
      </configuration>
    </plugin>
  </plugins>
  </build>

</project>
```

3. How Do We Configure the application. properties File with Information About the DB Used, the JPA/JWT, and Server Configuration?

We can configure the application.properties file with information about the DB used, the JPA/JWT, and server configuration, as shown in Listing 4-2.

Listing 4-2. The application.properties file

```
## DB Configuration ##
spring.datasource.url= jdbc:postgresql://localhost:5432/
jwtsecuritydb
spring.datasource.username= postgres
spring.datasource.password= postgres

## JPA / HIBERNATE  Configuration ##
spring.jpa.show-sql=true
spring.jpa.hibernate.ddl-auto=update
spring.jpa.properties.hibernate.dialect=org.hibernate.dialect.
PostgreSQLDialect
spring.jpa.generate-ddl=true
```

```
## Server Configuration ##
server.servlet.context-path=/api
server.port=8080
```

```
## JWT Configuration ## 256
jwt.jwtsecret = 2c503130819c59ec3fb959fa7e5aaa4ed39
d038367ad532ba36e5601f9baa77f4bcc36ca2b7a2e011d96c451cfec47
ef9997ccb3136e249186989d6e3eb0ea3ad40bda300e494210
4ba6e0cb1b8142eb33543dd4a589f545cacc86b29d3bb60918fb492471
337718f37ce1f2e8e352d309988ada4097df54f01c676b81b375129964db52
c3433044e0bb9adf809c80933b736d55cfaa36ba6a7799dfef229bc96cb6f
0c650ac8222519e607c5316044ac16342841630d1e2d74bd276cde4b
88e1b30f0a55622166f4863e704d4ec2e6fad367d3a67ddfc6354030e6a336
0f6989bc955296808d4f8c7ce0b48e268dda7dd33e3195c09c37ea2af068999
6427db
jwt.jwtExpirationTime = 36000000
```

4. How Do We Generate a JWTsecret Value for Our Project?

For our project I used the web app at https://jwtsecret.com/generate.

5. How Do We Create New APIs for Our Project?

In our Spring Boot JWT authentication example, we first register a new authorized user and then log in with username and password with the user's role "user."

The APIs included in our example are

Methods	URLs	Actions
GET	/api/public/welcome	Retrieve public content.
POST	/api/user/register	Register a new account.
POST	/api/user/authenticate	Log in an account.

6. How Do We Create New User and Role Models for Our Project?

Let's define our roles and define an enum called RoleName with the roles defined in Listing 4-3.

Listing 4-3. The RoleName class

```
package com.apress.JWT_Security_Authentication.models;

public enum RoleName {

    USER;

}
```

7. How Do We Create New Role Java Classes for Our Project?

Next, let's define the Role class as shown in Listing 4-4.

Listing 4-4. The Role class

```
package com.ons.securitylayerJwt.models;

import jakarta.persistence.*;
import lombok.*;
import lombok.experimental.FieldDefaults;
import org.springframework.security.core.GrantedAuthority;

import java.io.Serializable;

@Entity
@Getter
@Setter
@NoArgsConstructor
@AllArgsConstructor
@FieldDefaults(level = AccessLevel.PRIVATE)
public class Role implements Serializable  {

    @Id
    @GeneratedValue(strategy = GenerationType.IDENTITY)
    Integer id ;
    @Enumerated(EnumType.STRING)
    RoleName roleName ;

    public Role (RoleName roleName) {this.roleName = roleName;}
    public String getRoleName() {
        return roleName.toString();
    }
}
```

The Role class will simply create a table named "Role" with the authorized role such as "USER," which will be used to define the credential when registering a new user.

Finally, we create the User model class as shown in Listing 4-5.

Listing 4-5. The User model class

```
package com.apress.JWT_Security_Authentication.models;

import jakarta.persistence.*;
import lombok.*;
import lombok.experimental.FieldDefaults;
import org.springframework.security.core.GrantedAuthority;
import org.springframework.security.core.authority.
SimpleGrantedAuthority;
import org.springframework.security.core.userdetails.
UserDetails;

import java.io.Serializable;
import java.util.ArrayList;
import java.util.Collection;
import java.util.List;

@Entity

@Table(name = "users",
        uniqueConstraints = {
                @UniqueConstraint(columnNames = "firstName"),
                @UniqueConstraint(columnNames = "lastname"),
                @UniqueConstraint(columnNames = "email")
        })

@Getter
@Setter
@AllArgsConstructor
@ToString
@NoArgsConstructor
@FieldDefaults(level = AccessLevel.PRIVATE)
```

```java
public class User implements Serializable , UserDetails {

    @Id
    @GeneratedValue(strategy = GenerationType.IDENTITY)
    Integer id ;
    String firstName ;
    String lastName ;
    String email;
    String password ;
    String userRole ;

    @ManyToMany(fetch = FetchType.EAGER   , cascade =
    CascadeType.PERSIST)
    List <Role> roles ;

    public User (String email , String password , List<Role>
    roles) {
      this.email= email ;
      this.password=password ;
      this.roles=roles ;}

    @Override
    public Collection<? extends GrantedAuthority>
    getAuthorities() {
        List<GrantedAuthority> authorities = new ArrayList<>();
        this.roles.forEach(role -> authorities.add(new
        SimpleGrantedAuthority(role.getRoleName())));
        return authorities;
    }

    @Override
    public String getUsername() {
        return this.email;
    }
```

```java
@Override
public boolean isAccountNonExpired() {
    return true;
}

@Override
public boolean isAccountNonLocked() {
    return true;
}

@Override
public boolean isCredentialsNonExpired() {
    return true;
}

@Override
public boolean isEnabled() {
    return true;
}
}
```

Mainly, the User class will be used as a model to fetch the user credential and validate if it is not expired, locked, or enabled.

8. How Do We Create New Repository Java Classes for Our Project?

We will implement the repositories needed by each model we just created for persisting and accessing data. In a repository package, let's create two repositories:

UserRepository: To fetch the user repository info as shown in Listing 4-6

RoleRepository: To fetch the role repository info as shown in Listing 4-7

Listing 4-6. The UserRepository class

```
package com.apress.JWT_Security_Authentication.repository;

import com.apress.JWT_Security_Authentication.models.User;
import org.springframework.data.jpa.repository.JpaRepository;

import java.util.Optional;

public interface UserRepository extends
JpaRepository<User,Integer> {

    Boolean existsByEmail(String email);
    Optional<User> findByEmail(String email);

}
```

Listing 4-7. The RoleRepository class

```
package com.apress.JWT_Security_Authentication.repository;

import com.apress.JWT_Security_Authentication.models.Role;
import com.apress.JWT_Security_Authentication.models.RoleName;
import org.springframework.data.jpa.repository.JpaRepository;

public interface RoleRepository extends
JpaRepository<Role,Integer> {

    Role findByRoleName(RoleName roleName);

}
```

Let's configure now the Spring Security class named
"SpringSecurityConfig" in the security package as shown in Listing 4-8.

Listing 4-8. The SpringSecurityConfig class

```
package com.apress.JWT_Security_Authentication.security;

import lombok.RequiredArgsConstructor;
import org.springframework.context.annotation.Bean;
import org.springframework.context.annotation.Configuration;
import org.springframework.security.authentication.
AuthenticationManager;
import org.springframework.security.config.annotation.
authentication.configuration.AuthenticationConfiguration;
import org.springframework.security.config.annotation.web.
builders.HttpSecurity;
import org.springframework.security.config.annotation.web.
configuration.EnableWebSecurity;
import org.springframework.security.config.http.
SessionCreationPolicy;
import org.springframework.security.crypto.bcrypt.
BCryptPasswordEncoder;
import org.springframework.security.crypto.password.
PasswordEncoder;
import org.springframework.security.web.SecurityFilterChain;
import org.springframework.security.web.authentication.
UsernamePasswordAuthenticationFilter;

@Configuration
@EnableWebSecurity
@RequiredArgsConstructor
```

```java
public class SpringSecurityConfig {

    private final JwtAuthenticationFilter
    jwtAuthenticationFilter ;
    private final CustomerUserDetailsService
    customerUserDetailsService ;

    @Bean
    public SecurityFilterChain filterChain (HttpSecurity http)
    throws Exception
    { http
            .sessionManagement(session -> session.sessionCreati
            onPolicy(SessionCreationPolicy.STATELESS))
            .authorizeHttpRequests(auth ->
            auth.requestMatchers("/public/**", "/user/**").
            permitAll());

        http.addFilterBefore(jwtAuthenticationFilter,
        UsernamePasswordAuthenticationFilter.class);

        return  http.build();
    }

    @Bean
    public AuthenticationManager authenticationManager(Authen
    ticationConfiguration authenticationConfiguration) throws
    Exception
    { return authenticationConfiguration.
    getAuthenticationManager();}

    @Bean
    public PasswordEncoder passwordEncoder()
    { return new BCryptPasswordEncoder(); }

}
```

As this is the most important Spring Security class, let's explain it a bit more in detail:

1. **@EnableWebSecurity:** Allows Spring to find and automatically apply the class to the global Web Security.

2. Spring Security will load User details to perform authentication and authorization. So it has the `customerUserDetailsService` interface that we need to implement.

3. **PasswordEncoder:** Used for the AuthenticationProvider. If specified, it will use plain text.

4. The **(HttpSecurity http)** method is used from the WebSecurityConfigurerAdapter interface to tell Spring Security how we configure Cross-Site Request Forgery (CSRF) (disabled to send POST API), which filter (`jwtAuthenticationFilter`) and when we want it to work (filter before UsernamePasswordAuthenticationFilter), and which exception handler is chosen (`JwtUtilities`).

5. The implementation of `customerUserDetailsService` will be used for configuring AuthenticationProvider by the **AuthenticationManagerBuilder. userDetailsService()** method.

6. The URL path "/public/**" as a simple GET API will be permitted to all so that we can test a simple GET API with public content.

7. The URL path "/users/**" as a POST API will be also permitted to all so that all users can register and log in.

Listing 4-9 shows the `CustomerUserDetailsService` class.

Listing 4-9. The CustomerUserDetailsService class

```
package com.apress.JWT_Security_Authentication.security;

import com.apress.JWT_Security_Authentication.models.User;
import com.apress.JWT_Security_Authentication.repository.
UserRepository;
import lombok.RequiredArgsConstructor;
import org.springframework.security.core.userdetails.
UserDetails;
import org.springframework.security.core.userdetails.
UserDetailsService;
import org.springframework.security.core.userdetails.
UsernameNotFoundException;
import org.springframework.stereotype.Component;

@Component
@RequiredArgsConstructor
public class CustomerUserDetailsService implements
UserDetailsService {

    private final UserRepository UserRepository ;

    @Override
    public UserDetails loadUserByUsername(String email) throws
    UsernameNotFoundException {
        User user = UserRepository.findByEmail(email).
        orElseThrow(()-> new UsernameNotFoundException("User
        not found !"));
        return  user ;

    }

}
```

9. How Do We Create a JWT Authentication Filter for Our Project?

Now we need to create our JWT authentication filter and the authentication provider to make the security filter chain work.

The JwtAuthenticationFilter class, shown in Listing 4-10, will be used as a filter that executes once per request.

Listing 4-10. The JwtAuthenticationFilter class

```
package com.apress.JWT_Security_Authentication.security;

import jakarta.servlet.FilterChain;
import jakarta.servlet.ServletException;
import jakarta.servlet.http.HttpServletRequest;
import jakarta.servlet.http.HttpServletResponse;
import lombok.RequiredArgsConstructor;
import lombok.extern.slf4j.Slf4j;
import org.springframework.lang.NonNull;
import org.springframework.security.authentication.
UsernamePasswordAuthenticationToken;
import org.springframework.security.core.context.
SecurityContextHolder;
import org.springframework.security.core.userdetails.
UserDetails;
import org.springframework.stereotype.Component;
import org.springframework.web.filter.OncePerRequestFilter;

import java.io.IOException;

@Slf4j
@Component
@RequiredArgsConstructor
```

```java
public class JwtAuthenticationFilter extends
OncePerRequestFilter {

    private  final JwtUtilities jwtUtilities ;
    private final CustomerUserDetailsService
    customerUserDetailsService ;

    @Override
    protected void doFilterInternal(@NonNull HttpServletRequest
    request,
                    @NonNull HttpServletResponse response,
                    @NonNull FilterChain filterChain)
                    throws ServletException, IOException {

        String token = jwtUtilities.getToken(request) ;

        if (token!=null && jwtUtilities.validateToken(token))
        {
            String email = jwtUtilities.extractUsername(token);

            UserDetails userDetails = customerUserDetailsService.
            loadUserByUsername(email);
            if (userDetails != null) {
            UsernamePasswordAuthenticationToken
            authentication =
                    new UsernamePasswordAuthenticationToken
                    (userDetails.getUsername() ,null ,
                    userDetails.getAuthorities());
                log.info("authenticated user with email
                :{}", email);
            SecurityContextHolder.getContext().setAuthentication
            (authentication);

        }
```

```
        }
            filterChain.doFilter(request,response);
    }

}
```

JWT Authentication Filter

Let's explain a bit the JwtAuthenticationFilter class.

Now we will create the JWT service class we used in the class above.

First, we must check if the authorization header from our request is not null and it starts with the bearer word.

Next, if the request has JWT, we will validate it and parse username from it. We will extract our JWT from the authorization header and use a function from the JwtSecvice class called extractUsername to extract the value of the user email from the JWT.

Next, from username, we will use the "UserDetails" to create an Authentication object and set the current UserDetails in SecurityContext using the setAuthentication(authentication) method.

Finally, we send to get UserDetails:

```
UserDetails userDetails = customerUserDetailsService.
loadUserByUsername(email);
```

Let's create now the JwtUtilities class under the .security.jwt package where we will

- **Extract username from JWT**:
  extractUsername(String token)

- **Generate a JWT from email, date, expiration, and secret**

- **Validate a JWT**: Invalid signature, expired JWT token, unsupported JWT token, etc.

Listing 4-11 shows the JwtUtilities class.

Listing 4-11. The JwtUtilities class

```
package com.apress.JWT_Security_Authentication.security;

import io.jsonwebtoken.*;
import jakarta.servlet.http.HttpServletRequest;
import lombok.extern.slf4j.Slf4j;
import org.springframework.beans.factory.annotation.Value;
import org.springframework.security.core.userdetails.
UserDetails;
import org.springframework.stereotype.Component;
import org.springframework.util.StringUtils;

import java.time.Instant;
import java.time.temporal.ChronoUnit;
import java.util.Date;
import java.util.List;
import java.util.function.Function;

@Slf4j
@Component
public class JwtUtilities{

    @Value("${jwt.jwtsecret}")
    private String jwtsecret;

    @Value("${jwt.jwtExpirationTime}")
    private Long jwtExpirationTime;

    public String extractUsername(String token) {
        return extractClaim(token, Claims::getSubject);
    }
```

```java
public Claims extractAllClaims(String token)
{return Jwts.parser().setSigningKey(jwtsecret).
parseClaimsJws(token).getBody();}

public <T> T extractClaim(String token, Function<Claims, T>
claimsResolver) {
    final Claims claims = extractAllClaims(token);
    return claimsResolver.apply(claims);
}
public Date extractExpiration(String token) { return
extractClaim(token, Claims::getExpiration); }

public Boolean validateToken(String token, UserDetails
userDetails) {
    final String email = extractUsername(token);
    return (email.equals(userDetails.getUsername()) &&
    !isTokenExpired(token));
}
public Boolean isTokenExpired(String token) {
    return extractExpiration(token).before(new Date());
}

public String generateToken(String email , List<String>
roles) {

    return Jwts.builder().setSubject(email).
    claim("role",roles).setIssuedAt(new Date(System.current
    TimeMillis()))
            .setExpiration(Date.from(Instant.now().
            plus(jwtExpirationTime, ChronoUnit.MILLIS)))
            .signWith(SignatureAlgorithm.HS256, jwtsecret).
            compact();

}
```

```java
public boolean validateToken(String token) {
    try {
        Jwts.parser().setSigningKey(jwtsecret).
        parseClaimsJws(token);
        return true;
    } catch (SignatureException e) {
        log.info("Invalid JWT signature.");
        log.trace("Invalid JWT signature trace: {}", e);
    } catch (MalformedJwtException e) {
        log.info("Invalid JWT token.");
        log.trace("Invalid JWT token trace: {}", e);
    } catch (ExpiredJwtException e) {
        log.info("Expired JWT token.");
        log.trace("Expired JWT token trace: {}", e);
    } catch (UnsupportedJwtException e) {
        log.info("Unsupported JWT token.");
        log.trace("Unsupported JWT token trace: {}", e);
    } catch (IllegalArgumentException e) {
        log.info("JWT token compact of handler are
        invalid.");
        log.trace("JWT token compact of handler are invalid
        trace: {}", e);
    }
    return false;
}

public String getToken (HttpServletRequest
httpServletRequest) {
    final String bearerToken = httpServletRequest.
    getHeader("Authorization");
    if(StringUtils.hasText(bearerToken) && bearerToken.
    startsWith("Bearer "))
```

```
{return bearerToken.substring(7,bearerToken.length());
} // The part after "Bearer "
return null;
    }

}
```

Let's create now the TDO classes such as

- **BearerToken**: To set the bearer JWT token used in our example (Listing 4-12)

- **LoginDto**: Which is the Data Transfer Object for user login (Listing 4-13)

- **RegisterDto**: Which is the Data Transfer Object for registration of the user (Listing 4-14)

Listing 4-12. The BearerToken class

```
package com.ons.securitylayerJwt.dto;

import lombok.Data;

@Data
public class BearerToken {

    private String accessToken ;
    private String tokenType ;

    public BearerToken(String accessToken , String tokenType) {
        this.tokenType = tokenType ;
        this.accessToken = accessToken;
    }

}
```

Listing 4-13. The LoginDto class

```
package com.ons.securitylayerJwt.dto;

import lombok.AccessLevel;
import lombok.Data;
import lombok.experimental.FieldDefaults;

@Data
@FieldDefaults(level = AccessLevel.PRIVATE)
public class LoginDto {

    private String email ;
    private String password ;
}
```

Listing 4-14. The RegisterDto class

```
package com.ons.securitylayerJwt.dto;

import lombok.AccessLevel;
import lombok.Data;
import lombok.experimental.FieldDefaults;

import java.io.Serializable;

@Data
@FieldDefaults(level = AccessLevel.PRIVATE)
public class RegisterDto implements Serializable {

    String firstName ;
    String lastName ;
    String email;
    String password ;
    String userRole ;
}
```

Let's create now the Spring REST APIs Controller classes such as

- **PublicRestController**: A simple REST GET API with link "/public/welcome" for returning a Welcome message (Listing 4-15)

- **UserRestController**: Two REST POST APIs to register and log in a user, which will be explained more later (Listing 4-16)

Listing 4-15. The PublicRestController class

```
package com.apress.JWT_Security_Authentication.presentation;

import lombok.RequiredArgsConstructor;
import org.springframework.web.bind.annotation.GetMapping;
import org.springframework.web.bind.annotation.RequestMapping;
import org.springframework.web.bind.annotation.RestController;

@RestController
@RequestMapping("/public")
@RequiredArgsConstructor
public class PublicRestController {

    @GetMapping("/welcome")
    public String welcome ()
    { return "Welcome! This is a public content!" ;}

}
```

Listing 4-16. The UserRestController class

```
package com.apress.JWT_Security_Authentication.presentation;

import com.apress.JWT_Security_Authentication.controllers.
IUserService;
```

```
import com.apress.JWT_Security_Authentication.dto.LoginDto;
import com.apress.JWT_Security_Authentication.dto.RegisterDto;

import lombok.RequiredArgsConstructor;
import org.springframework.http.ResponseEntity;
import org.springframework.web.bind.annotation.PostMapping;
import org.springframework.web.bind.annotation.RequestBody;
import org.springframework.web.bind.annotation.RequestMapping;
import org.springframework.web.bind.annotation.RestController;

@RestController
@RequestMapping("/user")
@RequiredArgsConstructor
public class UserRestController {

    private final IUserService iUserService ;

    @PostMapping("/register")
    public ResponseEntity<?> register (@RequestBody RegisterDto
    registerDto)
    { return  iUserService.register(registerDto);}
    @PostMapping("/authenticate")
    public String authenticate(@RequestBody LoginDto loginDto)
    { return  iUserService.authenticate(loginDto);}

}
```

10. How Do We Create the Spring REST APIs Controller?

As explained earlier this REST APIs Controller UserService and its interface IUserService will be used to register a new user into the DB as well as log in the user.

As a final step, let's create the Spring REST APIs Controller (Listings 4-17 and 4-18) for authentication providing APIs for register and login actions such as

- api/user/register to:

    - Check the existing username/email.

    - Create a new User with role "USER."

    - Save User to the database using UserRepository.

- api/user/authenticate to:

    - Authenticate the email and password.

    - Update SecurityContext using the Authentication object.

    - Generate JWT.

    - Get UserDetails from the Authentication object.

    - Response contains JWT and UserDetails data.

Listing 4-17. The `IUserService` class

```
package com.apress.JWT_Security_Authentication.controllers;

import com.apress.JWT_Security_Authentication.dto.LoginDto;
import com.apress.JWT_Security_Authentication.dto.RegisterDto;
import com.apress.JWT_Security_Authentication.models.User;
import com.apress.JWT_Security_Authentication.models.Role;
import org.springframework.http.ResponseEntity;

public interface IUserService {
```

```
    String authenticate(LoginDto loginDto);
    ResponseEntity<?> register (RegisterDto registerDto);
    Role saveRole(Role role);

    User saverUser (User user) ;
}
```

Listing 4-18. The UserService class

```
package com.apress.JWT_Security_Authentication.controllers;

import com.apress.JWT_Security_Authentication.dto.LoginDto;
import com.apress.JWT_Security_Authentication.dto.RegisterDto;
import com.apress.JWT_Security_Authentication.dto.BearerToken;
import com.apress.JWT_Security_Authentication.models.User;
import com.apress.JWT_Security_Authentication.models.Role;
import com.apress.JWT_Security_Authentication.models.RoleName;
import com.apress.JWT_Security_Authentication.repository.
RoleRepository;
import com.apress.JWT_Security_Authentication.repository.
UserRepository;
import com.apress.JWT_Security_Authentication.security.
JwtUtilities;
import jakarta.transaction.Transactional;
import lombok.RequiredArgsConstructor;
import org.springframework.http.HttpStatus;
import org.springframework.http.ResponseEntity;
import org.springframework.security.authentication.
AuthenticationManager;
import org.springframework.security.authentication.
UsernamePasswordAuthenticationToken;
import org.springframework.security.core.Authentication;
import org.springframework.security.core.context.
SecurityContextHolder;
```

```java
import org.springframework.security.core.userdetails.
UsernameNotFoundException;
import org.springframework.security.crypto.password.
PasswordEncoder;
import org.springframework.stereotype.Service;

import java.util.ArrayList;
import java.util.Collections;
import java.util.List;

@Service
@Transactional
@RequiredArgsConstructor
public class UserService implements IUserService{

    private final AuthenticationManager authenticationManager ;
    private final UserRepository userRepository ;
    private final RoleRepository roleRepository ;
    private final PasswordEncoder passwordEncoder ;
    private final JwtUtilities jwtUtilities ;

    @Override
    public Role saveRole(Role role) {
        return roleRepository.save(role);
    }

    @Override
    public User saverUser(User user) {
        return userRepository.save(user);
    }

    @Override
    public ResponseEntity<?> register(RegisterDto
    registerDto) {
```

```java
if(userRepository.existsByEmail(registerDto.
getEmail()))
{ return  new ResponseEntity<>("email is already taken
!", HttpStatus.SEE_OTHER); }
else
{ User user = new User();
    user.setEmail(registerDto.getEmail());
    user.setFirstName(registerDto.getFirstName());
    user.setLastName(registerDto.getLastName());
    user.setPassword(passwordEncoder.
    encode(registerDto.getPassword()));
    String myrole = "user";

    if (registerDto.getUserRole().equals("") ||
    registerDto.getUserRole().equals("user")) {
        myrole = "USER";
    }

    Role role = roleRepository.findByRoleName(RoleName.
    valueOf(myrole));

    user.setUserRole(registerDto.getUserRole());

    user.setRoles(Collections.singletonList(role));
    userRepository.save(user);
    String token = jwtUtilities.
    generateToken(registerDto.getEmail(),Collections.si
    ngletonList(role.getRoleName()));
    return new ResponseEntity<>(new BearerToken(token ,
    "Bearer "),HttpStatus.OK);

}
}
```

```
@Override
public String authenticate(LoginDto loginDto) {
  Authentication authentication= authenticationManager.
  authenticate(
            new UsernamePasswordAuthenticationToken(
                    loginDto.getEmail(),
                    loginDto.getPassword()
            )
  );
  SecurityContextHolder.getContext().setAuthentication(
  authentication);
  User user = userRepository.findByEmail(authentication.
  getName()).orElseThrow(() -> new
  UsernameNotFoundException("User not found"));
  List<String> rolesNames = new ArrayList<>();
  user.getRoles().forEach(r-> rolesNames.add(r.
  getRoleName()));
  String token = jwtUtilities.generateToken(user.
  getUsername(),rolesNames);
  return "User login successful! Token: " + token;
  }

}
```

The last Java class we want to update is
JwtSecurityAuthenticationApplication, shown in Listing 4-19, where
we wish role "USER" to be populated automatically into the roles DB table.

Listing 4-19. The JwtSecurityAuthenticationApplication class

```
package com.apress.JWT_Security_Authentication;

import org.springframework.boot.CommandLineRunner;
import org.springframework.boot.SpringApplication;
```

```
import org.springframework.boot.autoconfigure.
SpringBootApplication;
import org.springframework.context.annotation.Bean;
import org.springframework.security.crypto.password.
PasswordEncoder;

import com.apress.JWT_Security_Authentication.controllers.
IUserService;
import com.apress.JWT_Security_Authentication.models.Role;
import com.apress.JWT_Security_Authentication.models.RoleName;
import com.apress.JWT_Security_Authentication.repository.
RoleRepository;
import com.apress.JWT_Security_Authentication.repository.
UserRepository;

@SpringBootApplication
public class JwtSecurityAuthenticationApplication {

    public static void main(String[] args) {
        SpringApplication.run(JwtSecurityAuthentication
        Application.class, args);
    }

    @Bean
    CommandLineRunner run (IUserService iUserService ,
    RoleRepository roleRepository , UserRepository
    userRepository , PasswordEncoder passwordEncoder)
    {return  args ->
    {   iUserService.saveRole(new Role(RoleName.USER));

    };}

}
```

The new project structure should look like Figure 4-5.

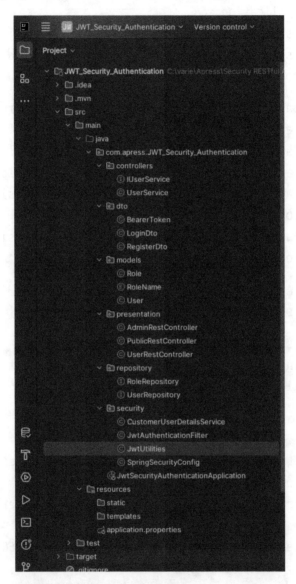

Figure 4-5. *Final Spring project structure*

Now that all the classes are generated, let's run and test our example:
`mvn spring-boot:run.`

11. How to Test Our Project?

First of all, let's download and install Postman testing tool at

`https://www.postman.com/downloads/`

Then install and run the tool as shown in Figure 4-6.

Figure 4-6. *Postman tool*

Let's test the `http://localhost:8080/api/public/welcome` to see that the public REST GET API works properly. Figure 4-7 shows the result using Postman testing tool.

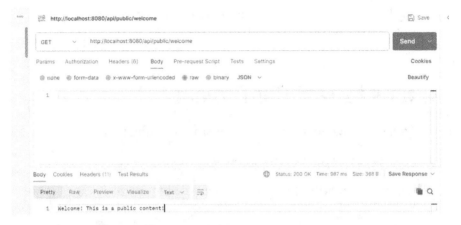

Figure 4-7. *Testing public REST GET API*

Next, let's register, via `http://localhost:8080/api/user/register`, a new user with role "USER" with the following credentials:

```
{
"firstName": "Massimo",
"lastName": "Nardone",
"email": "mmassimo@gmail.com",
"password": "masspasswd",
"userRole": "user"
}
```

Figure 4-8 will show the result in Postman.

Figure 4-8. *Registered a new user with "USER" role*

As you can see a new user is registered with status 200 OK and an access JSON Web Token is generated. The token type is Bearer. We can use that token to log in providing email/password and the JSON token just created now via `http://localhost:8080/api/user/authenticate`. Figures 4-9 and 4-10 show the result.

```
POST    ∨    http://localhost:8080/api/user/authenticate

Params   Authorization ●   Headers (9)   Body ●   Pre-request Script   Tests   Settings

  none   form-data   x-www-form-urlencoded   raw   binary   JSON  ∨

 1
 2   "email": "mmassimo@gmail.com",
 3   "password": "masspasswd"
 4
```

Figure 4-9. *Logging in the user with valid email/password*

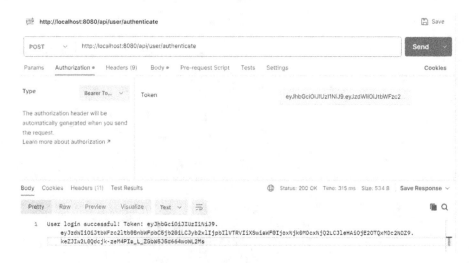

Figure 4-10. *Logging in the user with valid JWT*

Notice the status 200 OK, which means the user login is validated. Figure 4-11 shows the result if, for instance, we provide a wrong password.

Figure 4-11. *Forbidden login for a user providing a wrong password*

Summary

In this chapter, we showed you an example of how to secure a REST API using JSON Web Token (JWT) using Spring Security v6, Spring Boot v3+, and PostgreSQL DB. We explained how JSON Web Token works and finally provided a full example.

In the next chapter, we will show how to build a Securing OAuth2 Authentication application.

CHAPTER 5

Securing OAuth2 Authentication Flow

Spring Security is a highly extensible and customizable framework. Its flexibility stems from being designed with object-oriented principles and best practices, ensuring it is open for extension while remaining closed for direct modification. In the previous chapter, we explored a key extension feature of Spring Security—the ability to integrate various authentication providers. This chapter focuses on one of the most widely used authorization frameworks, Open Authorization 2.0 (OAuth 2.0). It will guide you through creating a secure login application using Spring Boot, Spring Web, and the OAuth2 client to connect with Google as provider.

RESTful APIs and OAuth 2.0

OAuth 2.0 is an authorization framework widely used to secure RESTful APIs, enabling third-party applications to access resources on behalf of a user without exposing their credentials. This makes OAuth 2.0 a critical component for building secure and scalable API ecosystems.

© Massimo Nardone 2025
M. Nardone, *Secure RESTful APIs*, Apress Pocket Guides,
https://doi.org/10.1007/979-8-8688-1285-9_5

OAuth2 Introduction

OAuth 2.0 (short for Open Authorization 2.0) is a widely used authorization framework that allows third-party applications to access a user's resources without exposing their credentials (such as usernames and passwords). It provides a secure and standardized way for users to grant limited access to their data or services to other applications or services, often referred to as "clients."

The key components of OAuth 2.0 are

- **Resource Owner**: The user who owns the data or resource

- **Client**: The application requesting access to the resource on behalf of the user

- **Authorization Server**: The server that authenticates the resource owner and issues tokens

- **Resource Server**: The API or server hosting the resource and validating tokens

It operates on the basis of tokens, which are short-lived and revocable access credentials. These tokens are used to authenticate and authorize access between the client application, the resource owner (typically a user), and the resource server (where the protected resources are stored).

OAuth 2.0 is widely used for securing APIs, allowing users to grant selective access to their data on platforms like social media, and enabling single sign-on (SSO) across different services.

Here's the typical flow about OAuth 2.0 operating through a token-based mechanism with RESTful APIs:

1. **Authorization Request:**

    - The client requests authorization from the resource owner, typically via a login screen provided by the authorization server.

2. **Authorization Grant**:

- The resource owner grants permission (e.g., through a consent screen) to the client.

3. **Access Token Issuance**:

- The authorization server issues an access token to the client if the grant is valid.

4. **API Request with Token**:

- The client sends the access token with each API request (usually in the authorization header as a bearer token).

5. **Token Validation**:

- The resource server validates the token with the authorization server or through introspection to confirm the client's access rights.

6. **Resource Access**:

- Upon validation, the resource server provides the requested data or performs the desired operation.

Here are the advantages of using OAuth 2.0 in RESTful APIs:

- **Decoupled Authentication and Authorization**: Allows third-party access without sharing credentials.

- **Granular Access Control**: Fine-grained permissions through scopes.

- **Improved Security**: Tokens reduce the risk of credential leakage.

- **Scalability**: OAuth 2.0 works seamlessly in distributed architectures.

OAuth2 Security

OAuth 2.0 provides a framework for authorization, but it is essential to implement it securely to protect user data and resources. Below are some key security considerations and best practices when using OAuth 2.0:

- **Use HTTPS**: Always use HTTPS to protect the communication between the client, authorization server, and resource server. This ensures the confidentiality and integrity of data transmitted during the OAuth flow.

- **Client Authentication**: Implement proper client authentication. Depending on the OAuth 2.0 flow being used, clients should authenticate themselves using client credentials or other methods like client certificates.

- **Authorization Code Flow**: For web applications and confidential clients, use the Authorization Code Flow. This flow involves an authorization code that is exchanged for an access token, reducing the risk of exposing tokens in the browser.

- **Token Storage**: Safely store and manage access tokens and refresh tokens on the client side. Avoid storing tokens in insecure locations such as browser cookies, and use secure storage mechanisms.

- **Token Validation**: When receiving access tokens from the authorization server, validate them properly. Check the token's signature and expiration date to ensure it's valid.

- **Scope Permissions**: Ensure that clients only request the minimum necessary scope of permissions (access rights) from the user. This principle is known as the principle of least privilege.

- **User Consent**: Always obtain clear and informed consent from the user before granting access to their data. Users should understand what data the client application can access and for what purpose.

- **Refresh Token Security**: Protect refresh tokens as they have a longer lifespan. Use secure storage and transmission mechanisms for refresh tokens. Only grant refresh tokens to confidential clients when necessary.

- **Token Revocation**: Implement token revocation mechanisms. Allow users to revoke access to their data and invalidate access tokens and refresh tokens when they are no longer needed.

- **Rate Limiting and Throttling**: Implement rate limiting and throttling to protect against brute-force and denial-of-service attacks on OAuth endpoints.

- **Cross-Site Request Forgery (CSRF) Protection**: Use anti-CSRF tokens or other techniques to protect against CSRF attacks that can trick users into making unintended requests.

- **Authorization Server Security**: Secure the authorization server against common security threats, such as injection attacks, and keep its software and libraries up to date.

- **Logging and Monitoring**: Implement comprehensive logging and monitoring to detect and respond to suspicious activities and security breaches.

- **Token Rotation**: Periodically rotate client secrets and access tokens to mitigate the risk of exposure due to unauthorized access or leaks.

- **Security Assessments**: Conduct security assessments, code reviews, and penetration testing to identify and address vulnerabilities in your OAuth 2.0 implementation.

The security of an OAuth 2.0 implementation depends on the combination of factors like the OAuth flow being used, the specific use case, and the client and authorization server configurations. Therefore, it's crucial to follow best practices, stay informed about security updates, and adapt your OAuth 2.0 implementation to the unique requirements of your application.

1. How to Integrate OAuth2 with Spring Security for RESTful APIs?

OAuth 2.0 can be integrated with Spring Security to secure your Java-based web applications, APIs, and microservices. Spring Security provides robust support for implementing OAuth 2.0 authentication and authorization in a Spring-based application.

Here's a basic overview of how to implement OAuth 2.0 using Spring Security:

- **Add Dependencies:** Ensure that you have the necessary dependencies in your project. Spring Security OAuth2 module is essential for OAuth 2.0 support. You can include it in your POM.xml or build. gradle file.

- **Configuration:** Configure Spring Security to handle OAuth 2.0 by creating a configuration class that extends AuthorizationServerConfigurerAdapter. This class should provide details about your OAuth 2.0 authorization server, client credentials, and endpoints. Listing 5-1 shows a configuration Java example.

Listing 5-1. Configure OAuth2

```
import org.springframework.context.annotation.*;
import org.springframework.security.oauth2.config.annotation.
web.configuration.*;
@Configuration
@EnableAuthorizationServer
public class OAuth2AuthorizationServerConfig extends
AuthorizationServerConfigurerAdapter {

    @Override
    public void configure(ClientDetailsServiceConfigurer
    clients) throws Exception {
        clients.inMemory()
            .withClient("client-id")
            .secret("client-secret")
            .authorizedGrantTypes("authorization_code",
            "password", "refresh_token")
            .scopes("read", "write")
            .redirectUris("http://localhost:8080/callback");
    }
}
```

- **User Authentication:** Configure how your application handles user authentication. You can use the default Spring Security mechanisms or integrate with external identity providers.

- **Resource Server Configuration (Optional):** If you're
  building an OAuth 2.0 resource server (e.g., an API),
  you'll need to configure Spring Security to validate
  access tokens. You can do this by creating a class that
  extends ResourceServerConfigurerAdapter. Listing 5-2
  shows a server configuration Java example.

Listing 5-2. Configure OAuth2 resource server

```
import org.springframework.context.annotation.Bean;
import org.springframework.context.annotation.Configuration;
import org.springframework.security.config.annotation.web.
builders.HttpSecurity;
import org.springframework.security.config.annotation.web.
configuration.EnableWebSecurity;
import org.springframework.security.web.SecurityFilterChain;

@Configuration
@EnableWebSecurity

public class SecurityConfiguration {

    @Bean
    SecurityFilterChain securityFilterChain(HttpSecurity http)
    throws Exception {
        return http
                .authorizeHttpRequests(auth -> {
                    auth.requestMatchers("/api/**").
                    authenticated ();
                    auth.anyRequest().authenticated();
                })
```

```
.oauth2Login(withDefaults())
.build();
}

}
```

- **Secure Endpoints**: Use Spring Security annotations like @Secured, @PreAuthorize, or @PostAuthorize to secure specific methods or endpoints in your application.

- **User Consent and Authentication Flow**: Implement a user interface for the OAuth 2.0 authentication flow. This includes handling user consent and redirecting users to the OAuth 2.0 authorization endpoint.

- **Token Storage and Management:** Implement token storage and management, including access tokens, refresh tokens, and their life cycles. Spring Security OAuth2 provides mechanisms to handle this.

- **Testing and Validation**: Thoroughly test your OAuth 2.0 implementation to ensure that the authentication and authorization flows work as expected. You can use tools like Postman or dedicated OAuth 2.0 clients for testing.

- **Logging and Monitoring**: Implement logging and monitoring to track security-related events and potential issues.

- **Documentation and Error Handling**: Provide clear documentation for developers using your OAuth 2.0–protected resources, and implement proper error handling to respond to various OAuth 2.0–related errors gracefully.

2. What Is OAuth2 Login?

OAuth 2.0 login is a secure and standardized way for users to grant permission to third-party applications to access their protected resources or perform actions on their behalf without sharing their login credentials. It is commonly used for single sign-on (SSO) and enabling users to log in to different websites or applications using their existing credentials from a trusted identity provider (IdP).

Here's what is included in OAuth2 login:

- **User-centric authentication**

- **Role of the user**

- **Authorization Code Flow**

- **Single sign-on (SSO)**

- **Third-party applications**

- **Scoped access**

- **Token-based authentication**

- **Security and authorization**

- **Widely adopted**

The OAuth 2.0 login feature lets an application have users log in to the application by using their existing account at an OAuth 2.0 provider (such as GitHub) or OpenID Connect 1.0 provider (such as Google). OAuth2 login can be also used to authenticate toward Facebook, Twitter, etc.

3. How to Develop an OAuth2 and Spring Security Project?

In our example we wish to configure a Spring authorization server with a social login provider such as Google and authenticate the user with OAuth 2.0 login, replacing the common form login.

Let's build our authentication and login application using Spring Boot 3, Spring Security 6, Spring Web, and OAuth2 Client.

The very first step is to create the Spring Boot Maven project using Spring Initializr, which is the quickest way to generate Spring Boot projects. You just need to choose the language, build system, and JVM version for your project, and it will be automatically generated with all the dependencies needed.

Navigate to `https://start.spring.io/` and use the Spring Initializr web-based Spring project generator to create the Spring Boot Maven project named OAuth2SecurityLogin, as shown in Figure 5-1.

Figure 5-1. *Generate an OAuth2 project using the Initializr web-based Spring project generator*

Select a Java v23 Maven project, using 3.4.0 Spring Boot version, and add the following dependencies: Spring Web and OAuth2 Client.

We will also add as dependency to the POM.xml file the Thymeleaf Java library, which is a template engine used to parse and transform the data produced by the application to template files. It acts just like HTML but is provided with more attributes used to render data.

Fill in all the required information and then click to generate the project. A project .zip file will be automatically generated. Download and unzip the file on your machine.

When opening the project with IntelliJ IDEA 2024.2.4, it will look Figure 5-2.

Figure 5-2. *Maven project structure*

4. What Are the Needed OAuth2 and Spring Security Dependencies?

The most important dependencies, which will be automatically updated in the POM.xml file, are shown in Listing 5-3.

Listing 5-3. Needed project dependencies

```
<dependency>
    <groupId>org.springframework.boot</groupId>
    <artifactId>spring-boot-starter-oauth2-client
    </artifactId>
</dependency>
<dependency>
    <groupId>org.springframework.boot</groupId>
    <artifactId>spring-boot-starter-web</artifactId>
</dependency>
```

The entire generated POM.xml file with the added dependencies is shown in Listing 5-4.

Listing 5-4. POM.xml file and dependencies

```
<?xml version="1.0" encoding="UTF-8"?>
<project xmlns="http://maven.apache.org/POM/4.0.0"
xmlns:xsi="http://www.w3.org/2001/XMLSchema-instance"
    xsi:schemaLocation="http://maven.apache.org/POM/4.0.0
    https://maven.apache.org/xsd/maven-4.0.0.xsd">
    <modelVersion>4.0.0</modelVersion>
    <parent>
        <groupId>org.springframework.boot</groupId>
        <artifactId>spring-boot-starter-parent</artifactId>
        <version>3.4.0</version>
```

```xml
    <relativePath/> <!-- lookup parent from repository -->
</parent>
<groupId>com.apress</groupId>
<artifactId>OAuth2SecurityLogin</artifactId>
<version>0.0.1-SNAPSHOT</version>
<name>OAuth2SecurityLogin</name>
<description>Demo project for Spring Boot Security and
OAuth2</description>
<properties>
    <java.version>23</java.version>
</properties>
<dependencies>
    <dependency>
        <groupId>org.springframework.boot</groupId>
        <artifactId>spring-boot-starter-oauth2-client
        </artifactId>
    </dependency>
    <dependency>
        <groupId>org.springframework.boot</groupId>
        <artifactId>spring-boot-starter-web</artifactId>
    </dependency>
    <dependency>
        <groupId>org.thymeleaf.extras</groupId>
       <artifactId>thymeleaf-extras-springsecurity6
        </artifactId>
        <version>3.1.1.RELEASE</version>
    </dependency>
    <dependency>
        <groupId>org.springframework.boot</groupId>
        <artifactId>spring-boot-starter-test</artifactId>
```

```
            <scope>test</scope>
        </dependency>
    </dependencies>

    <build>
        <plugins>
            <plugin>
                <groupId>org.springframework.boot</groupId>
                <artifactId>spring-boot-maven-plugin</artifactId>
            </plugin>
        </plugins>
    </build>

</project>
```

Let's build our first Java controller class named UserController, in Spring MVC, to specify its methods with various annotations such as the URLs of the endpoint, the HTTP request method, the path variables, etc.

Listing 5-5 will show the UserController Java class.

Listing 5-5. UserController Java class

```
import org.springframework.stereotype.Controller;
import org.springframework.web.bind.annotation.GetMapping;

@Controller
public class UserController {

    @GetMapping("/")
    public String homePage() { return "welcome";
    }

    @GetMapping("/welcome")
    public String welcomePage() {
        return "welcome";
    }
```

```
@GetMapping ("/authenticated")
public String AuthenticatedPage() {
    return "authenticated";
    }

@GetMapping ("/logout")
public String logoutPage() {
    return "redirect:/welcome";
}

}
```

The controller Java class will redirect to the welcome.html page for "/" and "/Welcome" and authenticated.html for "/authenticated" URLs. Logout mapping is used when logging out the user from Google authentication.

Let's create now two needed simple HTML pages as we did previously in this book:

- **welcome.html (Listing 5-6)**: A simple welcome page permitted to all users to provide the link to the authenticated.html page

- **authenticated.html (Listing 5-7)**: A simple HTML page showing the authenticated (Google) username if authenticated

Listing 5-6. welcome.html web page

```
<!DOCTYPE html>
<html xmlns="http://www.w3.org/1999/xhtml" xmlns:th="https://
www.thymeleaf.org">
<html lang="en">
<head>
    <meta http-equiv="Content-Type" content="text/html;
    charset=ISO-8859-1">
```

```
    <title>Spring Security 6 and OAuth2 Login authentication
    example!</title>
</head>
<body>

<div th:if="${param.error}">
    Invalid username and password.
</div>
<div th:if="${param.logout}">
    You have been logged out.
</div>

<h2>Welcome to Spring Security 6 and OAuth2 Login
authentication example!</h2>

<p>Click <a th:href="@{/authenticated}">here</a> to get
authenticated to Google with OAuth2 Login!</p>

</body>
</html>
```

Listing 5-7. authenticated.html web page

```
<!DOCTYPE html>
<html xmlns="http://www.w3.org/1999/xhtml" xmlns:th="https://
www.thymeleaf.org"
    xmlns:sec="https://www.thymeleaf.org/thymeleaf-extras-
    springsecurity6">
<head>
    <title>Spring Security 6 and OAuth2 Login authentication
    example!</title>
</head>
<body>
<h2>Welcome to Spring Security 6 and OAuth2 Login
authentication example!</h2>
```

```
<h2 th:inline="text">You are an authenticated user: <span
th:remove="tag" sec:authentication="name">thymeleaf
</span>!</h2>

<form th:action="@{/logout}" method="post">
    <input type="submit" value="Logout"/>
</form>

</body>
</html>
```

5. How to Create the Spring Security SpringSecurityConfiguration Java Class to Use OAuth2?

The most important Java class of the example, SpringSecurityConfiguration, is shown in Listing 5-8.

Listing 5-8. SpringSecurityConfiguration Java class

```
package com.apress.OAuth2SecurityLogin.configuration;

import org.springframework.context.annotation.Bean;
import org.springframework.context.annotation.Configuration;
import org.springframework.security.config.annotation.web.
builders.HttpSecurity;
import org.springframework.security.config.annotation.web.
configuration.EnableWebSecurity;
import org.springframework.security.web.SecurityFilterChain;
import static org.springframework.security.config.
Customizer.withDefaults;
```

```java
@Configuration
@EnableWebSecurity

public class SecurityConfiguration {

    @Bean
    SecurityFilterChain securityFilterChain(HttpSecurity http)
    throws Exception {
        return http
                .authorizeHttpRequests(auth -> {
                    auth.requestMatchers("/", "welcome").
                    permitAll();
                    auth.anyRequest().authenticated();
                })
                .oauth2Login(withDefaults())
                .formLogin(withDefaults())
                .build();
    }

}
```

The Spring Security Java class will

- Allow all users to access route "/" or "Welcome".

- Request any other request, like in our case "/
  authenticated", to be authenticated via Google.

- Use the OAuth2 login method to log in the list of the
  providers we listed into the application.properties file
  (in our case Google).

- Use the Spring Security v6 FormLogin.

6. How to Configure Google to Be Accessed via OAuth 2.0 Login?

The first step will be configuring the application properties file as shown in Listing 5-9.

Listing 5-9. application.properties configuration

```
# Google Login
spring.security.oauth2.client.registration.google.client-id=
<your-google-client-id>
spring.security.oauth2.client.registration.google.client-
secret= <your-google-client-secret>

# Configure Spring Security Logging
logging.level.org.springframework.security=TRACE
```

As we can see, by adding the line ...registration.google, we are telling Spring Security that we wish to access those social providers via OAuth 2.0.

7. How to Generate OAuth2 IDs and Secret Keys for Google?

To use Google's OAuth 2.0 authentication method for login, we must set up a project in the Google API Console to obtain OAuth 2.0 credentials (ID and secret) to be then added into the application.properties.

Let's follow these steps to generate the OAuth2 ID and secret key for Google:

1. Firstly, we must create a Google OAuth consent
    project and then link a consent to it. Let's visit the
    Google Cloud APIs & Services Console to create
    the project and the consent (Figures 5-3 and 5-4)
    at https://console.cloud.google.com/
    projectselector2/apis/credentials/consent?pl
    i=1&inv=1&invt=Abi-4w.

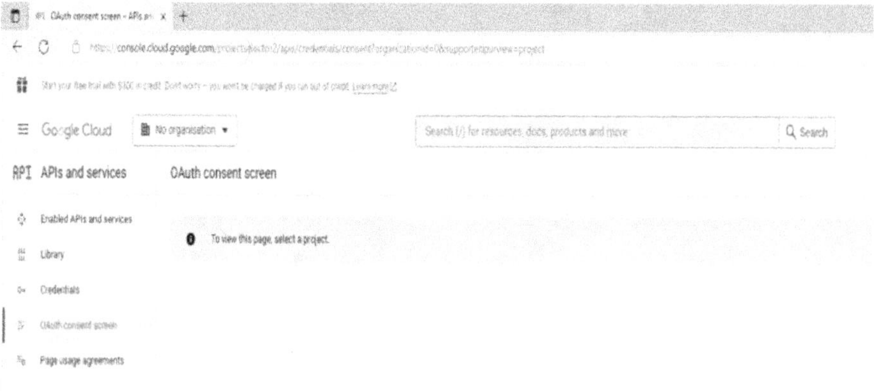

Figure 5-3. *The Google Cloud Console web page*

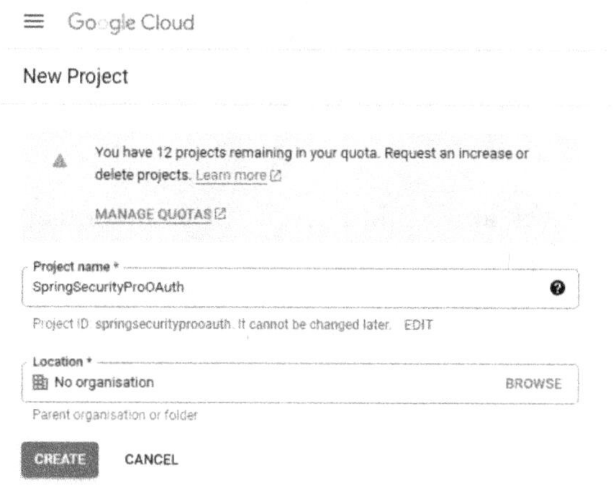

Figure 5-4. *The Google Cloud Console new project web page*

2. Now once the project is created, we can create a
    new consent associated to that project as shown in
    Figure 5-5.

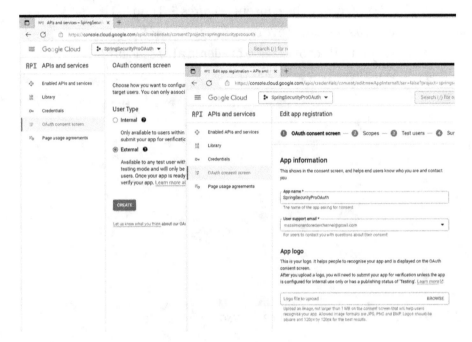

Figure 5-5. *The Google Cloud Console OAuth consent web page*

3. Next, go to the Credentials section and select Create
    OAuth 2 client ID.

    Select "Web application" as the type and enter a
    name for the application.

    Add the following as authorized redirect URI
    (Figure 5-6):

    ```
    http://localhost:8080/login/oauth2/
    code/google
    ```

4. Click "Create" to obtain your client_id and client_
   secret for our application.properties file as shown in
   Figure 5-6.

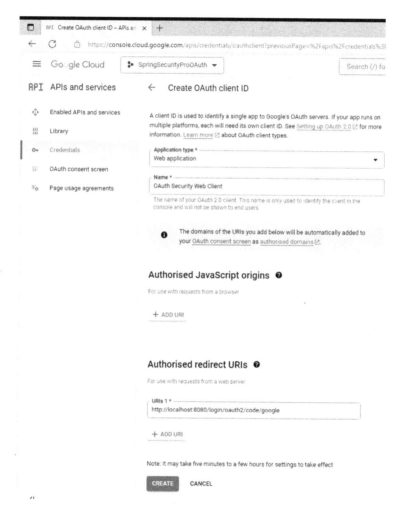

Figure 5-6. *The Google Cloud Console credential web page*

Figure 5-7 shows how the obtained client_id and
client_secret will be used for our application.
properties file.

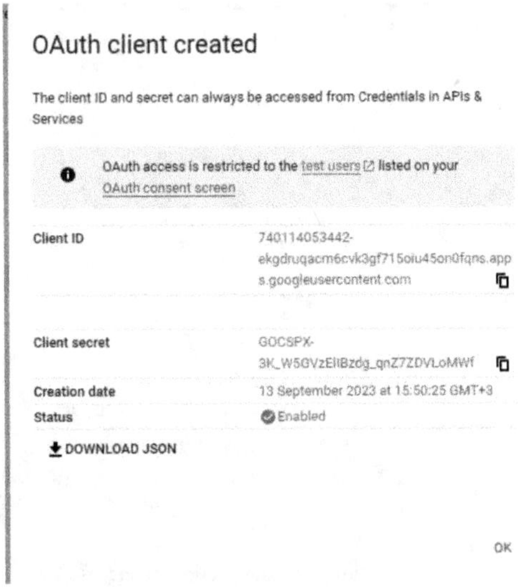

Figure 5-7. *The Google client_id and client_secret*

Copy the generated client ID and secret to our example application.
properties:

```
# Google Login
spring.security.oauth2.client.registration.google.client-
id= 740114053442-ekgdruqacm6cvk3gf715oiu45on0fqns.apps.
googleusercontent.com
spring.security.oauth2.client.registration.google.client-
secret= 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
```

The application is ready to be tested.

Run the application and visit `http://localhost:8080/welcome`. You
will see the `welcome.html` page shown in Figure 5-8.

Figure 5-8. *The welcome.html page*

Clink the "here" link to access the authenticated.html page, which will automatically redirect to the Spring login web page, which will provide the list, added in the application.properties of the social providers we are trying to access via the OAuth2 login authentication method as shown in Figure 5-9.

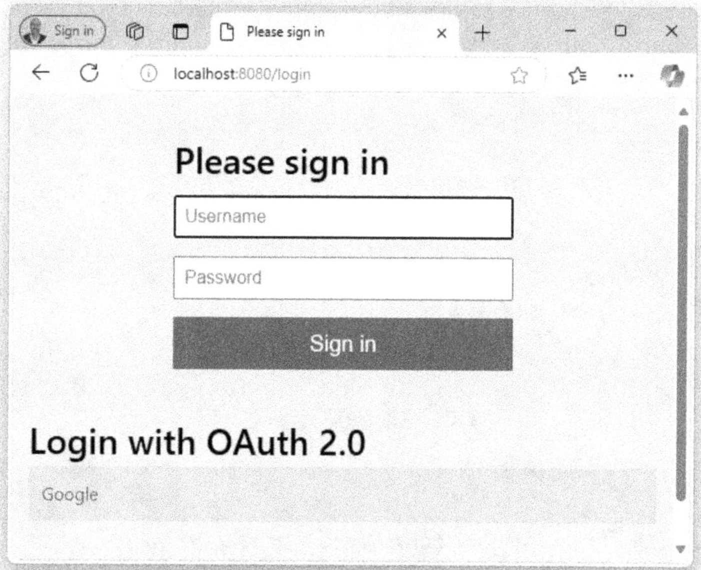

Figure 5-9. *The login web page*

Click the "Google" link, and you are then redirected to Google for authentication.

Next you will authenticate (Figure 5-10) with your Google account credentials, and you will see the consent screen, which will ask you to either allow or deny access to the OAuth Client you created earlier. You will click "Allow" to authorize the OAuth Client to access your email address and basic profile information.

Finally, the OAuth Client retrieves your email address and all the basic profile information from the UserInfo Endpoint that you configured in Google and establishes an authenticated session.

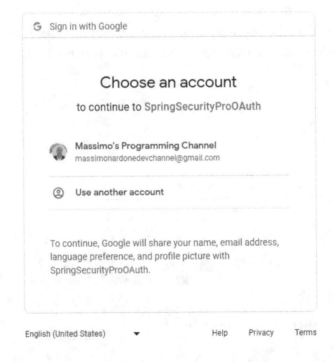

Figure 5-10. *The Google account selection web page*

If the Google client credential configured in the Spring application will match the Google OAuth configured ID and secret, then the user will be authenticated, showing the unique username, as shown in Figure 5-11; otherwise, a message error of not authenticated will be displayed.

Figure 5-11. *Google user is authenticated*

We successfully demonstrated how to configure OAuth2 login for Google.

Summary

In this chapter, we showed how Spring Security can be a very extendable and customizable framework as it is built using object-oriented principles and design practices so that it is open for extension and closed for modification. This chapter showed how to use one of the most used authorization frameworks named Open Authorization 2.0 (OAuth 2.0) and how to develop login security applications using Spring Boot, Spring Web, and OAuth2 Client (security) to authenticate toward Google as a provider.

Index

A, B

Application programming
    interfaces (APIs), 1
    definition, 2, 3
    HATEOAS, 3
    JavaScript Object Notation, 3, 4
    JWT authentication, 58
    RESTful APIs (*see* RESTful APIs)
    security techniques, 37
Authentication/authorization
    JWT (*see* JSON Web
        Token (JWT))
    OAuth 2.0, 91–117
    working process, 47, 48

C, D, E, F, G

Cross-Origin Resource Sharing
    (CORS), 17, 19, 21, 31
Cross-Site Request Forgery
    (CSRF), 66, 95

H, I

Hypermedia As The Engine Of
    Application State
    (HATEOAS), 3

Hypertext Transfer Protocol (HTTP)
    methods/verbs, 5–6
    status codes, 6–7

J, K, L

Java programming
    CustomerUserDetailsService
        class, 67
    repositories, 62–67
    role class, 58–62
    RoleRepository class, 63
    Spring Security class, 66
    SpringSecurityConfig class, 64
    user model class, 60
    UserRepository class, 63
JavaScript Object Notation (JSON),
    3–4, 11, 30
JSON Web Token (JWT)
    advantages, 48
    definition, 45
    header, 45
    JWT (*see* JWT authentication)
    payload, 46
    POM.xml files, 52
    signature, 46
    working diagram, 47, 48

© Massimo Nardone 2025
M. Nardone, *Secure RESTful APIs*, Apress Pocket Guides,
https://doi.org/10.1007/979-8-8688-1285-9

GPSR Compliance
The European Union's (EU) General Product Safety Regulation (GPSR) is a set
of rules that requires consumer products to be safe and our obligations to
ensure this.

If you have any concerns about our products, you can contact us on

ProductSafety@springernature.com

In case Publisher is established outside the EU, the EU authorized
representative is:

Springer Nature Customer Service Center GmbH
Europaplatz 3
69115 Heidelberg, Germany